Bedtime Stories
for Entrepreneurs

Inspiring Stories from
Clevelanders
Who Found Success

A COSE Publication

Written By
Karen Fuller, David Searls and Terry Troy

GREAT LAKES PUBLISHING
Cleveland, Ohio

ACKNOWLEDGMENTS

Publishing a book and starting a business have much in common: They start with a tiny spark in one person's mind; they take planning and an attention to detail that is unimaginable at the outset; and they require nurturing every step of the way. The entrepreneurs featured in this book rarely had many people to nurture their blossoming idea — they faced change and risk (and dare we say adventure), head-on and sometimes all alone. We, on the other hand, were lucky enough to have help from a surprising number of people on our own journey to create the book you hold in your hands, *Bedtime Stories for Entrepreneurs.*

We'd like to genuinely acknowledge the following individuals for their help in making this book a reality.

The spark for *Bedtime Stories* came from Steve Millard, executive director of COSE. Without his nurturing, this book would never have found its way into publication. His love for all things entrepreneurial was the driving force behind the idea for the book, along with the acknowledgment that there were great stories to be told about entrepreneurship in Northeast Ohio — someone just needed to find a way to tell them.

Special thanks to the COSE Board of Directors and Executive Committee, led by Jeanne Coughlin, COSE chairman, for championing this project. Your enthusiasm, support and encouragement on this inaugural book were invaluable.

Thanks to the COSE member volunteers who dedicated their time to pour over the list of more than 16,400 COSE-member companies and select the first 31 inspirational stories to feature in this book.

Thanks to Terri Kevany, senior director of communications and marketing at COSE, who took the idea of "an entrepreneurial book," shaped the vision, and led the charge to turn it into a reality.

Thanks to the COSE marketing team of Randy Carpenter, Jen Frimel, Jess Perko and Mark White and the committed support system of the entire COSE staff. Your efforts made for a final product of which every one of your colleagues can be proud.

Thanks to writers Karen Fuller, David Searls and Terry Troy for their exceptional ability to so elegantly and dynamically put to paper the collection of stories captured in this book. The trickiest part of this effort was finding ways to tell big stories in a few pages.

Thanks to the men and women of Great Lakes Publishing, including publishers Frank J. Bird II and Scott Lansky, who understood our vision and worked hard to bring it to life. To Steve Gleydura, Susan Hunter and copy editor Craig Gaines for their guidance, direction and expertise.

Thanks to artistic director Jennifer Dugan for her creative talents, Josh Hara for an inspired cover illustration and the entire team of skilled photographers: John Quinn, Walter Novak, Nannette Bedway, Jamie Janos and Izabela Viktoria.

And special thanks to editor Amber Matheson, who superbly managed the writing, editing and production of this book from start to finish. Your creativity and commitment were essential to its success.

And finally, we can't say "thank you" enough to each of the men and women featured in this book for trusting us to tell their personal stories of entrepreneurship. It's an honor and a pleasure to tell your tales.

COUNCIL OF SMALLER ENTERPRISES

ABOUT COSE

COSE, the small business arm of the Greater Cleveland Partnership, serves as a one-stop resource for its members by providing: group-purchasing programs that reduce the cost of doing business; education and development programs for small and mid-sized businesses; advocacy on legislative and regulatory issues affecting the business community; a wide range of resources focused on helping firms grow; and economic-development partners that can address business concerns. (www.cose.org)

CONTENTS

INTRODUCTION

I'm not sure when I realized we were different; after all, my family's experience was all I knew.

Before I was in grade school, my dad got laid off from his job in a sheet metal fabrication shop. Next thing I knew, we were in the newspaper business — delivering them on a rural route in Pennsylvania. Every morning my brother and mom went one direction, my dad and I the other. I was the folder, bander and bagger. Learning came quickly … a random newspaper to the head reminded me to duck as we approached the subscribers who lived on the right side of the route.

Dad got another regular job, but the side work is always what I remember best. Most kids I knew had a garage with an assortment of tools, toys and other junk. Our garage was a machine shop with a drill punch, a brake press and a sheet metal sheer. Dad made parts for Model A's that we delivered to a guy in a tough part of Philadelphia who supplied them to restoration shops and hobbyists.

Mom, with a high school education and paralegal training, worked with a friend to open a school for paralegals — from scratch. Later, our basement became Mom's office, where she did the billings from Dad's night and weekend metal fabrication work and transcribed courtroom proceedings and legal dictation.

Of course, they pursued other opportunities— I especially remember assembling and packaging motorcycle jumper cables at the kitchen table. Still later, in the early '80s, when gas soared to more than $1 a gallon, Dad came home with an old 800-gallon-tank truck. We painted a name on the side and became "Heritage Home Kerosene." I can still clearly recall some bitter cold winters in that old truck, pumping kerosene into five-gallon cans in the church parking lot after Mass or in the local five-and-dime lot on Saturdays.

Eventually Mom got a degree and became a high school teacher and administrator. Dad had a heart attack that prompted his most significant "entrepreneurial seizure" — finally deciding he'd be his own boss. He started a carpet-binding business in the early '90s and is successfully retiring from that business this year.

We never got rich or famous and no one wrote my parents' entrepreneurial stories. But they had an impact on me. From Junior Achievement companies in high school to the first small business I ever started, in college, they taught me an appreciation for independence, a tolerance for risk and a desire to create something better for myself and my family. It is that appreciation for everything entrepreneurial that brought me to lead the Council of Smaller Enterprises.

Small business owners make a tremendous impact. They affect not only their own friends and families, but their communities as well. Today, more than half of the working population in the United States is employed by smaller businesses. I could list dozens of facts and figures, statistics and economic conclusions, but the bottom line is that net new-job creation in the U.S. is driven by entrepreneurs. Small business is at the core of this country's economy. As small businesses go, so goes the economy.

At one point or another almost everyone considers being their own boss, building their own thing or doing something better than their boss can. What differentiates the folks in this book from most is that they actually did it. They risked their future and the future of those dependent on them to chase an idea, pursue a dream or create something that did not exist before. Some of them did it intentionally or by necessity, and some ended up entrepreneurs by chance or legacy.

We think it's important to tell stories such as these, not only to provide inspiration for those who may be inclined to try their hand at entrepreneurial success, but also to recognize and celebrate the entrepreneurs in these pages as well as others whose stories have not yet been told. In Cleveland, throughout Northeast Ohio, and across the country, these people and their businesses are making an impact every day in small and big ways.

These 31 stories share the same sense of courage and spirit that my parents' story embodies for me; we hope you find inspiration, humor and kinship in the entrepreneurial adventures of your fellow Northeast Ohioans.

Steve Millard
Executive Director
The Council of Smaller Enterprises

1

LIVING THE

DREAM

The One Ocean ...

... 60 hours a week,
350 players a day and
$2.56 that changed
Danny Vegh's life forever.

Pop quiz. You get three guesses, and the first two don't count. Name the local Cleveland businessman who came to the United States determined to achieve his American Dream, plus fame, fortune and glory, on a thunderous wave of pingpong paddles and pool tables.

If you said Danny Vegh, you've done your Cleveland Business 101 homework.

He fled the Soviet tanks rumbling into Hungary during the communist invasion in the mid-1950s and arrived in America with just a change of underwear and a pingpong paddle. It would take him very little time to become a top-ranked pingpong player and one of the biggest showboats around.

A fellow Cleveland player, Earl Nittskoff, remembers a storybook-perfect tale of Vegh's talent. A hotshot player, a young hustler, called out Vegh. By this time he was in his 30s, retired from the pro circuit. "This kid was ranked the No. 2 player in the country, easily, and he came up from Columbus to play Danny," says Nittskoff. "The kid bets him $200 that he could beat him, a lot of money back then. Danny took his money and the kid sat on the steps and cried."

Vegh wanted to make it. Period. He wanted out from under the thumb of a communist regime. He wanted choices. And unlike a proper little communist boy, he wanted to be in charge.

"As a kid, after the communists took over, we visited a factory and they asked, 'What do you want to be?' I said, 'Director of the factory.' They took us to an opera house and I told them I wanted to be director of the opera."

Vegh has never had a problem believing in his own abilities. He arrived in New York City speaking only his native tongue, but he wasn't in Hungary anymore, and he certainly wasn't looking backward.

So he moved to Cleveland on a tip from the consular office in New York that our little corner of the United States had a large Hungarian population. Worked 60 hours a week in a factory. Learned English at the library. Rented an apartment with eight light bulbs and called his mother to tell her.

"They literally had a dirt floor where he came from," says his daughter, Kathy Vegh. "He didn't have his first light bulb at home until he was 6."

He was living the American Dream, from the bottom up.

He realized pingpong wasn't quite as popular here as it had been back in Hungary, but instead of quitting the game he'd conquered, the former Hungarian National Junior Ping Pong Champion just Americanized it a little: He started to showboat.

New school meets old school: Kathy Vegh and her father, Danny Vegh.

DANNY VEGH'S BILLIARDS & HOME
Entrepreneurs: Danny Vegh and daughter, Kathy Vegh
Founded: In 1963 Danny opened a table tennis club; Danny Vegh's three stores grew out of that business.
Employees: 46

He could keep four balls in play at once, serve from behind his back or between his legs, head-butt it like a soccer ball, catch it with his lips, and return a serve at competition speeds approaching 55 mph. Try it sometime.

His skills got him noticed. That paddle and little white ball took him through 48 national television appearances in the '60s, including more than a dozen stints on "The Tonight Show" with Steve Allen and "The Mike Douglas Show." He traveled the country with a partner, putting on exhibitions. It was a classic rags-to-riches story: "The national wage was $1 [an hour]," he recalls. "If you were an engineer or a teacher, you made maybe $4,000 [a year], OK? The Cleveland Browns started at $9,000. They paid me 12."

Vegh had riches, fame, a green card … then he pushed his luck, and his dream, a little too far. It wasn't enough for him to see his new countryside as a star. He wanted to own his own business: the final piece of the American Dream.

He sunk $8,000 ("Everything I had, plus …") into a 10,000-square-foot table tennis club where he'd committed to a monthly rent of $700. In the wee hours of August 20, 1963, at the end of his first 16-hour workday that generated a grand total of $2.56, he realized that pingpong may not be the way to retire.

"I thought I'd commit suicide," he says with a chuckle.

But he kept on trying, and made a living, of sorts, for two years. He offered pricey private lessons and added a few pool tables beside the pingpong tables to bring in a little more business. A table's a table, right?

It turned out those pool tables weren't just any old tables: Pool was happening. Paul Newman was "The Hustler," and the pool halls were just seedy enough that moms didn't want their boys hanging out there, which meant that many of them hung out there, cigarettes dangling from their lips.

So Danny moved to a classier joint in the old Hippodrome Building on Euclid Avenue and started a pool hall that drew 350 players a day, seven days a week. On the side, he started to sell a few tables, a little equipment here and there.

Of course, he played the game, too. Nothing like table tennis, but he didn't embarrass himself with a stick. Eventually he came to a realization that would affect the rest of his life: The best players made the worst owners. Too many pool hall owners were "concentrating on their game, not the business," he says. "I put down the cue stick and didn't play for 10 years. I was not in it for fun. I was in it to make my living."

In 1979 he opened his landmark store on Lorain Avenue, and the rest is Cleveland history. Today, Vegh's spunky daughter, Kathy, is the one in the spotlight, marking the full evolution of a 50-year vision. In 2004, the so-called "tornado" (Danny's word) decided they could go bigger, do better, sell more. She convinced her dad to buy a store in Mayfield Heights that would cater to the well-heeled East-siders who got lost trying to make their way to Lorain Avenue. It was operating in the black in less than 30 days.

Her dad stayed away during the renovation process of his daughter's store, and only saw the completed Mayfield Heights site when he arrived at the grand opening in March 2005. The paint was barely dry when the Veghs hosted well-dressed politicos, friends, family members, business associates and other hustlers and notables. The liquor flowed, the crowd feasted on Hungarian food and swayed to a 10-piece band. Danny Vegh started dreaming in an apartment with eight light bulbs. He finally accepted his success in the showroom of his daughter's store.

"He had tears in his eyes," says Kathy.

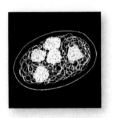

If You Cook It, They Will Come

Grandma's recipes are a universal favorite, and you grew up learning how to cook them. Imagine sitting across the street from your family's business, watching everyone else re-create her dishes, while you waste away at a desk. Sometimes, you just have to go home.

Growing up in the small Italian enclave near St. Rocco's on Cleveland's near West side, Joe Santosuosso never envisioned himself running the family's restaurant business.

"It was just a small neighborhood bar and restaurant back then," says Joe. "It was not even close to what it is now."

Founded by his grandmother Louise, the small restaurant and bar started as Louise's Garden, but became Johnny's after World War II, when Joe's father, Eugene, and uncle John came back from the war.

"My dad and uncle decided on Johnny's because it was a lot easier to say than Eugenio's," says Joe.

That little family business has grown into a Cleveland icon, and much of that growth can be attributed to Joe.

Joe, along with brothers John and Anthony (Bo), grew up in the business. Joe worked in the kitchen alongside his father and mother, Francis, whom he credits with teaching him his culinary skills. Not content to stay in the family business, Joe went away to college and received a business degree from Ashland University.

His first job after graduation took him even farther away. He landed a position with Owens-Illinois, which sent him to Pennsauken, N.J.

But Cleveland and the old Fulton Road neighborhood were never far from his mind. In fact, a spring manufacturing company just across the street from Johnny's on Fulton, Reliable Spring, recruited Joe. Eventually he accepted the offer. Looking across the street at the old family business each day, Joe grew nostalgic for his days in the kitchen. That's when he started to cook again, and that's when the new Johnny's was born.

Joe gave Johnny's on Fulton an attitude adjustment. Sautéed veal dishes and unique pastas were added to the menu. The wine list quietly went upscale. But the changes came slowly, by design, so as not to upset the popular neighborhood restaurant's existing clientele.

That was more than two decades ago. Today, Johnny's comprises four locations. The old neighborhood restaurant on Fulton is still there, and the family has added three locations downtown: Johnny's Bistro, Johnny's Downtown and Johnny's Little Bar.

Johnny's has become a haven for Cleveland's elite. It's not unusual to see local and even national celebrities dining there. But Joe is not the kind to be star-struck.

"They come for the food," he says flat-out. "They may get a nice table, and I'm

Joe Santosuosso stands in the new incarnation of Louise's Garden, the patio at Johnny's on Fulton.

sure some of our servers may treat them a little differently, but it's our goal to treat everyone like they are special."

So how did a small Italian neighborhood restaurant evolve into one of Cleveland's premier upscale eateries? For the locals who watched the many changes occur through the years, the more interesting question is, "Why?"

"My brothers and I were getting bored with just running a tiny corner bar," says Joe. "So we started playing with it. For me, it started out as a hobby. I started cooking at Johnny's on Fulton one day a week, then two, then three. Before I knew it, they were lined up in the street and people were sitting in the stairwells waiting for tables."

Then one fall Saturday in the early 1980s, Dick Jacobs (former owner of the Cleveland Indians) and locally known commercial realtor Dominic Visconsi showed up.

"And we didn't have a table for them," says Joe. "I knew who they were, of course, and I'm saying, 'What am I going to do?' And they're standing there looking at all these people in our bar wondering what the hell is going on. That's when I knew we had made it. Since then, they have both become good friends. But they couldn't even get in the door back then."

But the initial changeover didn't sit well with many in the old Fulton Road neighborhood, where Johnny's had been a staple for some 80 years. Johnny's always served good food, but it was much more reasonably priced when it was a neighborhood establishment. Today's entrees start in the teens and can surpass $30, while a Friday-night fish fry in the '70s cost around $6.

"That's why we did things slowly," says Joe. "Some of our regular customers weren't really that happy with what we were doing, and I knew they wouldn't be. We did things slowly because we didn't want to scare anyone. Even today, when we get some old-timers in — if we get the little couple from down the street that's coming in for a fish fry on a Friday night — they will still pay what they used to pay. Some of them don't even know our new prices exist."

Making the changeover to an upscale eatery also created some friction among the brothers, Joe admits.

"You always have sibling rivalry, but that's something you always have in a family business," he says. "Bo and I even had a small fight today. You have to be able to let things roll off your back like water. And the person who's wrong has to know when to admit it and back down."

Today, Bo and Joe remain involved in the business they grew up with, along with a nephew, John, and their partner, Paul Anthony. Joe's parents, Eugene and Francis, live in Florida, but Francis still comes back for an occasional taste test.

"And she always has something to say," says Joe.

Founder Louise died four years ago.

"I remember growing up in the kitchen, when we'd get busy, we would pound on the ceiling with a broom handle and my grandmother would come down from her upstairs apartment to help us out," says Joe. "She'd be pushing people out of the way, showing everyone how to do things. She was a great lady."

While it retains much of its old charm, Johnny's on Fulton has changed, of course. The most recent upgrade is a dining patio, appropriately called Louise's Garden.

JOHNNY'S
Entrepreneurs: Joe, John and Bo Santosuosso
Founded: Grandma Louise set up shop in the early 1930s. Her sons Eugene and John took it over and made it Johnny's after WWII. Their sons Joe, John and Bo officially took over in 1974.
Employees: 100-plus, depending on the season

"Sometimes I think I can still hear her walking around out there," says Joe. "It's a lot different from the business she founded, but I think she would like what we've become."

Daisy Knows Best

Adele Malley **inherited** an entrepreneurial spirit from her father. But it was her mother who **taught** her all the things she could do with it.

I t's been a sweet life for Adele Malley — she's a wife, a mother and a recent retiree from her position as president and CEO of Cleveland's most well-known and well-loved candy company: Malley's Chocolates. But it's also been a life of hard lessons.

Adele was born a Ryan; she didn't know much about the candy industry until she married into it. "Bill, of course, grew up in the candy business," she says of her husband. "But I grew up in a family business, too." Her father, Bill Ryan, ran the Bill Ryan Provision Co. on East Fourth Street and Bolivar Avenue, "which now is right about second base at Jacobs Field," Adele notes. "He catered to the ships on the Great Lakes and local restaurants." Her father died when Adele was in the sixth grade, forcing her mother, Adele "Daisy" Ryan, to make a decision she really wasn't prepared to face.

Left with a fledgling meat-packing business, $7,000 in cash, four children to raise and no formal business training, Daisy decided to make a go of it.

The tragedy brought the family closer together, says Adele. "She had always been more of a socialite than a businessperson. And she didn't really have a mathematical background, either. She was also the only woman around. She would come home at night and tell us everything that happened to relieve some of her stress. And we would all sit there and listen; it was all so interesting."

It soon became more than just dinner conversation. When Adele was in seventh grade, Daisy took her to collect an overdue bill.

"She drove me over to a restaurant and said, 'Now Adele, these people owe us money, but they are going to tell you that they can't pay us because they're not doing very well. But we have bills to pay, too,'" Adele remembers. "'So I want you to go in there and tell that lady who you are and I'll be right here in the car, and when that lady at the cash register tells you she can't pay you, you tell her that we'll just take $10 or $15. And that way I'll stop in every week until they pay that bill.'"

She was a shy, preteen girl, but Adele did what her mother told her and soon brought back the $10 payment.

"There was the lesson that even though someone owed you money, you should find different ways of helping them in doing what is right," says Adele. "[The owner] could have paid $2 a week, and I'm sure mother would have taken that. Mother was always thinking about other people and their comfort, but she mixed it with business sense."

Observing how Daisy worked, and how she solved problems in business and life, had a profound impact on Adele's life.

Adele Malley shows off the sweet stuff. The medal around her neck signifies her status as a Master Emeritus Confectioner. The pin on her lapel is from her 2004 induction into the National Confectioner's Sales Association Candy Hall of Fame.

"Like if you don't feel like going to work, just get up, get dressed and get in there," says Adele. "After you start to work, you begin to forget yourself."

When Adele married Bill and started a family of her own, she started passing on those life lessons to her children.

Even though they were very young when Malley's opened its North Olmsted store, Adele would sometimes take the children in with her when she worked.

"It was Palm Sunday and we were busy for Easter," Adele remembers. "I had to be there to help out."

MALLEY'S CHOCOLATES
Entrepreneurs: Bill and Adele Malley
Founded: In 1935 by Mike and Jo Malley. Their son William (Bill) Malley, stepped in as president in 1967. His wife, Adele, became president in 1996 after Bill retired.
Employees: 257-325, depending on the season

So, kids in tow, Adele went to the store. While she was busy helping customers, she gave the boys the job of filling bags with Easter-basket grass.

"They had a machine that would melt the bag together at the top," she says. "Naturally, most of the bags came out lopsided, or not filled all the way, or some of the grass was burnt, but we just

Malley's Chocolates

explained to our customers what was going on. We gave away the bags for free, but we never told the children. They thought they were contributing."

Often, the Malley kids would ride along with Bill to ring out the stores after closing. "Bill would load them all into the station wagon and head down to check out the store registers," says Adele. "The store was closed and the lights were subdued, so it really had a magical feel. The children would all sit there eating their treats. I think that's when our children really started to become aware of how much fun our business is."

A sense of the importance of family infused the Malley business from the very beginning, when Jo joined her husband, Mike, in the original shop. It continued with their son Bill's deep respect for his own wife. "I married a fellow who was so comfortable in his shoes, he was always pushing me into the limelight," she says. "The husband-and-wife thing worked because he was so open in letting me go with my thoughts — I have many friends where the family wouldn't allow the daughter-in-law to shine, and I didn't find that at all in the Malley family." Today, four of their six children still work in the shop, including the newest president, Dan Malley.

"This is such a friendly business," she says. "Think about it: When people come into one of our stores, they are usually doing something nice for someone — buying a present for someone's birthday, or wedding, or baptism. We are very happy to have surrounded ourselves with this kind of life."

A life filled with the sweet and bittersweet, forged in the lessons she learned from a strong, ready-for-anything woman named Daisy.

The *Hottest* Business in Cleveland

One guy from Mississippi figured he had a line on great ribs. Luckily for Lemaud, he didn't have to do it on his own — he had four brothers who believed in his dream *and* were willing to work for free.

Fats Domino, Mudcat Grant, Mike Tyson, Steve Harvey, The O'Jays and American Idol Ruben Studdard probably know more about Hot Sauce Williams than the typical suburban Clevelander, but there are parts of the city where the Williams clan is as well known as the Stokes brothers ever were. Construction workers, Cleveland Clinic docs, night owls and respectable, churchgoing folk looking for Sunday carryout all pay tribute to these barbecue chicken and rib barons by providing a steady influx of business at their three area restaurants.

"Just say 'Hot Sauce' and one of us will answer," says Jim Williams, one of five brothers behind the popular local restaurant chain.

The "Hot Sauce" label fell into their laps.

"We didn't name ourselves; our customers did," says Jim.

It was a passing of the torch; the title belonged to a previously untouchable rib guy who'd run a Cleveland rib joint years before the Williams crew came cookin'.

The nothing-fancy eatery was the between-jobs inspiration of Lemaud Williams, the baby of the family, back in 1964. Like his parents and four brothers, Lemaud had migrated up from Tougaloo ("between two creeks"), Miss., where they do ribs right.

Tougaloo is basically a small college campus with a scattering of housing along its edges. "Most of the black doctors in Mississippi graduated from Tougaloo College," says Jim, who also attended the school before, years later, finishing up with a business administration degree from Kent State University.

The town was mostly black, including the school's faculty, but Jim remembers playing with the few white kids whose parents worked there. Their father did construction, and food was always on the table. None of the three surviving brothers has anything bad to say about their hometown.

But Tougaloo was only seven miles from Jackson. Different story. The bus into the big town had reserved seating for blacks.

"It was degrading," Jim recalls. "We'd get off maybe three miles before we got to Jackson so we wouldn't get insulted and assaulted when the bus pulled into town."

There were no jobs for blacks in the late 1940s, even — or especially — for a man with a college education. One after another, most of the Williamses settled in Cleveland.

Things were better here, as long as Jim didn't try to use that degree he finally earned in 1954. He was in the Army awhile, got married, had a couple kids, found

Hot Sauce is still a family affair; from left, Mike, Sharon, Essie, Deborah, Jim, Lemaud, Alan and Herb Williams.

office jobs here and there, and eventually bought a small house that he and wife Jean still own in the workingman's section of Shaker Heights.

In 1958, he began teaching at R.B. Hayes High School and eventually moved to East Madison Elementary.

His brothers, meanwhile, settled in at the Armour meat plant and elsewhere. Life went on like that until the day in '64 when ringleader Lemaud needed a job and wanted no part of working for anyone else. He knew how to do hot 'n' spicy, and figured he had a market.

Jim Williams chuckles and holds his hands two feet apart when describing the size of that first location. "It had a sink," he says.

There wasn't nearly enough money in the venture for everyone to take home a paycheck, so everyone besides Lemaud had two gigs: one for cash, one for family.

"Some worked days, some worked nights," says Jim.

So while one brother was reporting in to the restaurants, another might be checking out for a quick snooze before clocking in on the paying job. Jim, being a teacher, spent his summers taking the Hot Sauce Williams trailer to fairs, picnics and rib burnoffs.

Hot Sauce Williams

"They pretty much took over the state fair in Columbus," says longtime customer Clyde Johnson, who remembers "the longest lines on the fairgrounds" in front of the Hot Sauce Williams booth.

The otherwise-employed brothers wouldn't take a penny out of the business.

"But as we opened up another location, one more brother would leave his job to run it," Jim recalls.

In the mid-'60s they opened a location at East 75th Street and Euclid Avenue, across from Leo's Casino. The legendary nightclub drew Stevie Wonder, B.B. King, The Supremes, John Coltrane and other blues, soul, jazz and Motown legends. Many of them ended up at the restaurant after the last show, as did their fans. Word got around.

"[Jazz singer] Nancy Wilson used to send for our sauce," says Herb. "I had to get her some to take back to California."

Fats Domino once spent several evenings after performances at one Hot Sauce location. "[Restaurant employees] knew he was someone, and they all tried to guess who. He didn't tell them till his last night," says Jim.

Iron Mike Tyson ate there, and used to date a niece in the Williams family.

Despite all the late-night action, the restaurants have rarely had any trouble. Even the rare law-breaking served as a backhanded compliment. One miscreant was apprehended during an after-hours break-in. "He was still in there eating chicken and ribs when the police came and got him," Jim recalls.

It turns out Lemaud really *did* know hot 'n' spicy; what they really need a security system for is the secret sauce recipe. Essie Williams, Bill's widow, tells of getting a phone call from someone who wanted to start a Hot Sauce franchise operation in Detroit. When told that the family wasn't interested, he replied that all he really needed was that recipe. Naturally, he was turned down.

"He told me he could figure it out anyway," says Essie with a cackle. As long as there's a Williams family member dedicated to serving up ribs and protecting the family recipe, that's not likely to happen.

HOT SAUCE WILLIAMS
Entrepreneurs: Brothers Lemaud, Alonzo, Jim, Bill and Herbert Williams
Founded: Lemaud opened the first restaurant in 1964. Today the company is run by the surviving Williams brothers, Lemaud, Jim and Herbert, and by Bill's widow, Essie Williams.
Employees: 75-80

Piece Work

Meet Joe.

He was 14, just moved here from a rough neighborhood in Brooklyn.

He was a hard worker and a good kid ...
Watch how he systematically put all the parts of his career together to become one of the most successful small business owners in Cleveland.

Joe Lopez grew up in Brooklyn, New York, in a rough Italian neighborhood where his was the only Latino family he knew. Eventually, the Lopez family escaped that environment and moved to Canton, Ohio, where some family friends were part of a growing Latino community.

Once settled in Canton, Joe kept busy with school and work. He always had a job and liked to learn. One lesson he would learn repeatedly throughout his career was that people who own businesses get all the good perks — flexibility, control, money. He saw his father working long hours in construction, and he knew there had to be a better way.

A trip to Colorado to visit some high school friends presented Joe with an opportunity that focused his life's path. What was supposed to be a two-week stay turned into a two-and-a-half-year learning experience.

His first job out West was working as a lumberjack for two young entrepreneurs. That summer, Joe saw firsthand the benefits of entrepreneurship. "I remember doing all the heavy lifting, and a lumberjack does a lot of really heavy lifting," he says. "And I'd see my bosses — two young guys — taking it pretty easy, choosing what they wanted to do, going home when they felt like it."

Joe left lumberjacking, but stayed in Colorado in a position that took him back to his roots: construction, his father's profession. He was building commercial properties, learning the trade as a union laborer. It proved a valuable experience. "All the time I worked there, I was watching and learning," says Joe. "I wanted to figure out exactly how the guys in charge were doing everything — planning the jobs, managing the workers — there's really a lot to it." Joe realized a few other things during his time there: He enjoyed construction, he was good at it and it was in his blood.

Joe loved Colorado, but missed his family. It was time to get back home and settle down.

Back in Canton, Joe got a job at an engineering firm learning skills such as wiring, inlay work and routing that would prove valuable behind the scenes in the building industry. He liked the work, but was also intrigued by another job option; during that time he was moonlighting as a waiter with Continental Restaurant Systems and making more money waiting tables. His good work got the attention of higher-ups at the Canton-based company, and they offered to train him for management.

Joe Lopez takes a break from "only working half the day — seven to seven!"

Joe chose money and responsibility, and the chance to earn another piece of his career puzzle. He excelled in the management-training program, moving up the ranks as a trainee, then as a manager, then as a trainer.

"As a trainer I learned the business aspects of running a restaurant," Joe says. His training led him to a career traveling to restaurants that were in the red and helping them get back into the black. After about five years, he was ready to move on, taking with him valuable management and problem-solving skills.

The next plot in his map was a job selling industrial-maintenance chemicals in the late '80s: He picked up people skills, negotiation know-how and the ability to close a deal.

"That was really the last piece I needed," says Joe. "I learned about salesmanship — how to create a need and fill that need. I also learned about industrial sales and how to deal with companies in Cleveland." Joe was the top-producing salesman year after year, starting

> **NEW ERA BUILDERS INC.**
> **Entrepreneur:** Joe Lopez
> **Founded:** The company was officially incorporated in 1989.
> **Employees:** More than 30

New Era Builders Inc.

with only two accounts in his territory and ending his career there with 330 accounts. "They loved me there," Joe says. "I was making excellent money at a young age, and really becoming a successful salesman." But as usual, Joe could see that it was his boss, the owner of the company, who was taking trips to Maui every year and reaping the benefits of Joe's sweat equity.

With his skill-building finally complete, Joe began branching out on his own while keeping his lucrative day job.

He started to buy real estate in areas including Lakewood, Cleveland and West Park. He fixed up houses, resold them and reinvested the money into more properties. When he got tired of that, he started constructing premanufactured homes, and New Era Builders was born.

New Era quickly became too big a job to handle part-time, and Joe took the plunge he'd been priming for his entire life: He quit his high-paying sales job and began to nurture his own business.

"Throughout my career I had been seeing signs that being a business owner is where the real benefits are, so there was no question that it was what I wanted to do," he says. But after several years, building homes for people began to lose its appeal and challenge. That's when Joe's business took a turn for the better.

Someone had defaulted on building a Burger King Restaurant, and Joe took on the unfinished job. After finishing in only 31 days, he was immediately awarded another contract. After that, three more commercial contracts had New Era's momentum cruising at a very comfortable pace. "Since then, I've never looked back," Joe says. Today, his clients include Case Western Reserve University, NASA Glenn, the U.S. Coast Guard, the city of Mentor, the city of Cleveland ... the list goes on and on. He put in his time, learned every piece of the entrepreneurial puzzle, and today he couldn't be happier. "I always wanted to make a civic and social contribution, to make a good living wage and to be able to provide for others," he says. "We have done all those things."

So what's his favorite part of being a business owner? "Only working half the day — seven to seven," he laughs.

2

ROLLING

THE DICE

The Symbiotic
Brewmasters

How about a **simple** three-step
approach to success?
First, help your **neighborhood**.
Second, help your **city**.
Third, help the **whole world**.
After a couple of beers, it doesn't
sound *that* impossible.

When Pat and Dan Conway signed the initial lease on the building that would house Great Lakes Brewing Co., they decided to come to Market Avenue for a visit with their wives. What they found was a donnybrook, a melee of street people complete with jabs, haymakers and broken bottles. "Our wives said, 'My God! What have you gotten yourselves into?' " Pat remembers. That was in 1988.

"We're thinking of expanding even more over there," he says today, pointing toward the brewery from the Brewing Co.'s beer garden.

"My brother and I, being mutual optimists … said, 'Look at the upside. This neighborhood couldn't get any worse.' My momma raised a fool — but not that big a fool. We realized that we had two solid anchors with the West Side Market and St. Ignatius. So this neighborhood really had a lot of upside to it. And I think that we absolutely did the right thing. Now we own the buildings and we do nothing but establish one more expansion event after another," he says.

After Great Lakes Brewing set up shop, other businesses followed suit. The Market Avenue Wine Bar opened in 1994, followed by the Flying Fig restaurant in 1999 and Talkies Café in 2000. These days, Market has become the place for a romantic evening stroll or an afternoon brunch, rather than a street brawl.

Inside the Brewing Co., there was even more activity taking place. The brothers were intent on creating a microempire at a time when many people hadn't even heard the term "microbrewery." And, by the way, they wanted it to be completely environmentally friendly, too.

"It was a pretty novel idea at the time," Pat says of their brewing scheme. "When we first opened, there were about three-dozen breweries in the country. Now there are 1,400."

What they found as they learned about the industry was that much of the byproducts from the brewing process were simply thrown out. And that, for the Conways, was just unacceptable.

"We have a very strong commitment to the environment," says Pat. "We are changing the paradigm as to how we operate our business. Instead of 'take, make, waste,' we are now, 'take, make and remake.' "

The tons of barley used during the brewing process is given for free to local dairy farmers who then convert it to feed. The spent grain also finds its way into the hands of local artisan bakers who use it to make pretzels and gourmet breads.

"Another portion of the grain is given to Killbuck Farms, who turn it into a

Patrick, left, and Daniel Conway stand in the heart of it all, the brewery at Great Lakes Brewing Co.

substrate for growing organic mushrooms," he adds.

Mistakes in the bottle-filling process aren't given away to employees or the public — despite our pleadings during brewery tours.

"We can't legally sell anything less than 12 ounces if the bottle says 12 ounces," Pat explains. "We don't even give the low-fills away to our staff, because they deserve 12 fluid ounces as well."

But rather than pour the low-fills down the drain, the beer is used to make sauces, soups and glazes in the company's restaurant.

The brothers approach every aspect of their business with an attitude that asks "How can we make it better?"

"We were one of the first establishments in Ohio to go non-smoking," says Pat. "We read reports on secondary smoking that said that it's not so much our customers who are at risk, people who come in here maybe weekly or monthly, but it's our employees who are at risk. We thought it was the right thing to do. Even though it may have a negative impact on our business, we thought we would just let the chips fall where they may."

But it didn't have a negative impact. In fact, sales at the restaurant and brew pub grew 10 percent after the no-smoking policy was implemented.

"I think people like our courageous side," says Pat, who credits his parents with

Great Lakes Brewing Co.

providing the brothers with their strong socially responsible underpinning. "We enjoy our environmental approach to things and we also have a strong corporate-responsibility component of our mission statement. We always give back to the community who supports us."

And lately, it's not just Cleveland giving the brewery support. "The market is embracing our product," says Pat. "In the fourth quarter, according to the scanning information we are getting from the Neilsen company, the top-selling beer in Northeast Ohio is not Bud, not Miller and not Coors. It's Great Lakes Christmas Ale." Their beers routinely win national, regional and local awards, and their brewery has a reputation as one of the finest in the United States.

Meanwhile, Pat and Dan have quietly begun to launch an initiative that has the potential for national and global reach. In summer 2005, they celebrated their fifth-annual Burning River Fest.

The festival isn't focused on celebrating any of the Great Lakes award-winning brews. Rather, the day-long event features music, locally grown and prepared food and exhibits from area environmental groups in an effort to raise awareness of larger issues. The Conways want to raise the environmental consciousness of the community, celebrate organic farmers and homegrown food, and point out the need for better water quality.

"All the profits from the festival went to support EcoCity Cleveland, a charity which will use that money to talk about issues such as water quality," says Pat.

Eventually, the Conways hope the Burning River Fest will become to environmental festivals what Newport has become to jazz or Sundance has become to film.

"In the early '70s, when our river caught fire, rivers were catching fire all over the world," says Pat. "But that event spurred a lot of legislation which helped clean up our nation's rivers."

So why not, they thought? Why not irreverently brew the Burning River Pale Ale, throw a whole party to discuss why rivers *shouldn't* catch fire, and get a bunch of beer-lovers to see how easy it is to care about the environment?

Let's see: Reinvigorate the neighborhood and make it a prime location for new businesses? Check. Help the city by recycling *and* making great beer? Check. Save the world? They're working on it ...

GREAT LAKES BREWING CO.
Entrepreneurs: Brothers Pat and Dan Conway
Founded: 1988
Employees: 75-100 depending on the season

Be Cool

In the event of a fire, move quickly
but calmly to the exits. Stay composed,
take control of the situation and lead others
to safety. The same rules apply for would-be
entrepreneurs building a company.
Success can often be determined by your
own reaction to a little heat in the kitchen.

During the young life of Beachwood-based BrandMuscle Inc., there have been at least two crises that might have left other companies in ashes. But other companies weren't run by Phil Alexander.

"He is never low. He's so ebullient," says Bonnie Skuggen, the company's HR manager and one of its first employees. "It's not that Phil doesn't show fear; he doesn't feel it."

Phil, the son of an Indian diplomat, found his way to Northeast Ohio and his wife, Linda, by way of Sri Lanka, Sweden and other exotic points. Stress is supposed to age a person, so one might assume that the youthful-looking CEO has led a charmed existence. You wouldn't guess that he's had to sell a product that didn't exist to a roomful of executives from a Fortune 500 corporation. Or that there came a point when there wasn't enough cash in the company checking account to meet payroll.

"He never panics," says Skuggen.

It was in the late 1990s that Phil, then vice president of marketing for Pearle Vision in Twinsburg, went shopping for a software solution to a common problem.

Theoretically, a corporation's creative types design an ad and send it to hundreds or thousands of branch offices or retail outlets so they can customize it to local markets — namely, addresses, phone numbers, site-specific sales info, etc.

In reality, someone on the local level accidentally reruns the summer sale ad in October. Or a franchisee's brother-in-law expresses his interest in graphic design by donating a brand-new logo and color palette. Or a corporate marketing intern sends the version with Iowa's fine-print state regulations to Idaho.

If you're a marketing director of a large corporation, it's enough to make you pull out your hair and become a closet drinker of stomach-coating medication.

Unless you're Phil Alexander, in which case you search for the automation that must exist to let corporations keep certain elements in central control while allowing fool-proof local customization. When you don't find it, you see an opportunity. "If you can logically explain it, you can write code," you fervently believe. You know just enough digital technology from your days as a computer lab assistant at Case Western Reserve University to be dangerous and intuitively believe the marketplace will embrace your vision and that investors will give you money.

"I hadn't ever asked anyone for a million dollars before," Phil recalls with a smile. But he found a Boston investor, and headed to Beantown.

Perhaps wisely choosing the day *after* April Fools' Day 2000, Phil's BrandMuscle became one of the first of 23 startup tech companies housed in his investor's incubator. His advisers were smart and helpful. They went to work, and just three weeks later ran into their first "crisis."

Phil Alexander is respected around the office for keeping his cool, and around the area for bringing his company back home to Ohio.

It was a potentially panic-inducing prospect: A major corporation wants your pitch, and you've got no logo, no sales materials and — oh yeah, no product.

"We were three weeks into brainstorming," Phil recalls. "We hadn't written a line of code. I didn't even have a business card."

A former business associate had dropped an offhand remark that would spur a frenzy of activity. She had a vague idea of what Phil was up to, and mentioned it to someone at AT&T Wireless. BrandMuscle was immediately invited to make a presentation.

"This was on a Thursday, and we had to meet with them the next Tuesday," says Phil.

There was no fallback date — the occasion was a rare gathering, in New Jersey, of group heads. Phil, his acting CFO, and a former college roommate acting as a consultant mocked up a logo and printed business cards and stationery at a nearby copy center.

Then the harried team threw together a laptop presentation. They needed an existing ad to use as a template to demonstrate the embryonic software, and arbitrarily chose one from Bell Atlantic Wireless. They removed all identifying characteristics and referred to it as "ABC Wireless."

On Monday — the day before the presentation —Maria Santoferraro, Phil's

BrandMuscle Inc.

former co-worker from a company called Brand Target Optical, joined the team. Not the best of circumstances for a new employee, but Maria shrugs it off.

"I think if Phil told me, 'Let's open a hot dog stand,' I'd do it." She's still with BrandMuscle as vice president of client services.

Phil's people struggled to get the laptop presentation working properly. On Tuesday, they decided to drive to Jersey rather than fly, just to buy some time.

They were greeted by about 15 serious-minded marketing reps. Sure enough, the presentation failed at some points. Then a team member accidentally referred to the demo ad as Bell Atlantic Wireless.

"Everyone in the room sort of sucked in their breath," says Phil, who, in the uncomfortable silence that followed, had time to imagine being escorted out by security. But after a little nervous laughter, the pitch continued.

Afterward, the AT&T execs conferred in private.

"When they came out they said, 'We'll go forward, but only if we can get it before Bell Atlantic,' " Phil recalls with a chuckle.

He was so stunned that the demo had been mistaken for work in progress on behalf of a competitor that he was unprepared for the next question: What would it cost?

Phil stammered that BrandMuscle would have to do a needs assessment.

Someone asked if there was a charge for the service, and Phil's consultant responded quickly, "Yes. $50,000."

Done, said BrandMuscle's first client.

Imagine your HR manager warning you that there's $6,000 in the checking account. You're no math major, but you know eight full-time employees do not equal the cash on hand. You won't make payroll. Let's see you stay cool now.

"I was never as nervous as I should have been," says Bonnie Skuggen, who delivered the bad news, about her confidence in top management.

Slightly misplaced confidence, possibly.

"We were just racing through cash," Phil admits.

His tech people were creating something from nothing. And that first sale to AT&T Wireless had been an anomaly. Nearly a year later, they were still waiting to hook their second customer.

"Everyone thought I had all this money, but I couldn't have been poorer," says Phil.

He'd been chasing the company's next round of investment for months, but the bubble had burst. "Investors were being a lot more careful, a lot slower to respond."

Despite the economy, Phil got approval from a venture-capital firm for a

$5 million cash infusion in mid-March 2001. They were one signature away. All they required was a signoff from their CFO — who was in Israel. Somewhere.

While they desperately attempted to track down their financial officer, Phil called a special meeting and told the staff his pockets were empty. Paychecks would be delayed. He didn't have nearly enough in his personal accounts to cover everyone, but he promised to help anyone in desperate straits as much as he could. They could see him in his office after the meeting.

"Not a single person stopped in," says Phil, still stunned at that vote of confidence.

Soon afterward, the wayward CFO was found, papers were faxed and the checking account was replenished.

Today, BrandMuscle employs 80. The company has a roster of Fortune 500 clients for whom it custom-designs technology that makes their ads conformable to endless variations in size and content. Phil Alexander is seen by many as a local hero for returning his company to Beachwood when Boston beckoned.

And if — or when — the economy sours again, there will likely be little grumbling or hastily updated resumes. When your CEO stays cool, so does everyone else.

> BRANDMUSCLE INC.
> **Entrepreneur:** Phil Alexander
> **Founded:** 2000
> **Employees:** 80

HEINEN'S

Trend Chasers in *Aisle Five*

Cultural patterns are shifting to confront third-generation supermarket owners Jeff and Tom Heinen. The brothers face two annoyingly conflicting trends in the marketplace, and fight their battle as one of the last of a dying breed: a family run, local chain of grocery stores. But the Heinen family doesn't run from change or challenge.

Jeff Heinen, left, and his brother Tom have run Heinen's together since 1994.

I
t was 1929, just before the '20s stopped roaring and the Great Depression set in. Joseph Heinen went into business for himself after managing a butcher shop for an owner who rejected his idea of adding a few grocery items to the product mix.

"We're butcher-shop people," Joe was told in so many words. "Why would we sell food? That's for grocers."

But Joe, who'd astutely perceived that housewives of his day might appreciate the chance to take care of two shopping trips in one store, took the revolutionary step of selling bread, milk and a few other staples along with the family pot roast at his shop in Shaker Heights.

He was the first local grocer to embrace the self-serve approach, and he opened Cleveland's first real supermarket in 1933.

What the family patriarch couldn't have seen coming were the conflicting trends of consumers with decreasing time and burgeoning selection that have created a new generation of headaches, and opportunities, for his grandchildren, Jeff and Tom Heinen. The twin brothers oversee a 16-store chain with locations throughout Northeast Ohio; they're little fish in a big pond with big obstacles to overcome.

Heinen's

"We had 268 feet of grocery gondolas [shelving units] back in the 1980s," says Tom. "Today we have 460 feet." The reason?

Customers see television commercials for a new patented-formula laundry detergent, and they have to have it. They seek out the extra-strength, lite, low-sodium, fat-free, organic, recycled or new-and-improved versions of their favorite brands.

"It used to be, 'Here's the tomato sauce,' " Tom recalls. Not anymore. "You've got tomato sauces, and tomato sauces with mushrooms, and tomato sauces with mushrooms and peppers ..."

It's called line extension, an ingenious strategy in which a manufacturer can release a slightly modified version of a tried-and-true brand, create customer demand and effectively force retailers to carry it.

Take ketchup. One brand comes in six sizes. "We mostly sell one size, but if a customer is looking for another and it's not there, they're disappointed," says Tom. "They want what they want, when they want it. I candidly admit that I don't think I'm any different."

Tom also admits, as a divorced father of two teenage daughters, to being as squeezed for time as the rest of us. So he understands the reasoning behind the other trend hitting U.S. supermarkets.

"Every Saturday in the Pepper Pike store where I worked as a 15-year-old, the [checkout] lines went from the registers back to the back wall where the frozen cases were. Two-cart orders were nothing. Sometimes you'd see three and even four carts."

Contrast this with today's scene: Consumers run in to grab an armload of quick-prep items for the night's meal before picking up the kids from school.

"People fragment their shopping," says Tom, who points out that nowadays the 12-items-or-less checkout lane tends to be the busiest. "They now shop more often, buy fewer items per trip, and use the other channels more often."

Ah, those other channels. They're everywhere: convenience stores, gas stations, pharmacies and even the big-box retailers, which can make for a convenient stop if the shopper is already there on another mission. And don't forget the fast-food

---

HEINEN'S
Entrepreneurs: Brothers Jeff and Tom Heinen
Founded: In 1929 Joseph Heinen opened his first butcher shop, which would eventually become Heinen's. His grandsons Jeff and Tom assumed joint leadership upon the death of their father, Jack Heinen, in 1994.
Employees: About 2,300

joints and restaurants.

The Heinen brothers have responded in a number of ways. The chain has a long-established reputation for service and quality, and their people are now better trained in customer relations and product than ever.

"You need to be an expert because there aren't people at home focusing on food," Tom explains.

A lesser-known advantage is the store's prices. Tom says shoppers are always surprised to see that Heinen's comes in lower than most area competitors on most products. That's an important piece of info for shoppers who trek the miles of aisles at a price-squeezing superstore to find deals on toilet paper and aspirin.

But the brothers are really focusing on that time-and-selection conundrum. They've responded with a sort of science experiment that they call Heinen's Village Market.

While the Wal-Marts and the Kmarts and the national supermarket chains have beefed up in an attempt to gobble the market, the location the Heinen family opened in April 2005 in Hudson is bucking this trend. Heinen's Village Market is less than one-third the size of the company's Avon location. The balance was struck on the side of efficiency over selection.

"In 20,000 square feet, we have the items that represent about 80 percent of what most grocery stores sell," Tom says. "We don't carry every available size, and shoppers might find that we don't have their Hunt's ketchup brand, but we carry Heinz."

Is it a fair trade-off? Will this neat, petite model satisfy customers' need for speed? Or will it scare away shoppers who can only find the 16-ounce can and not the 12-ounce version of their favorite brand of peaches?

The jury's still out. While early sales figures were slightly down at the svelte store, Tom Heinen says that he's found, anecdotally, an "overwhelmingly positive reaction from shoppers." If the concept works, there might very well be a whole chain of Village Markets in the company's future.

Who knew it would be this hard to keep a successful, established company successful and established? It makes us want to just grab a six-pack and a frozen dinner and forget about it.

Will that be a light beer or full-bodied? Import or domestic? Low-sodium dinner or fat-free? He-man or regular?

Cotton Chameleon

In an industry that's had its fair
share of change, there are a few
leaders who've become masters
at adapting. Of course, it helps
when your childhood coincides
with growth spurts in your
family's fledgling business.

Alan Rosskamm sees the future, and it's changing every day.

F or Alan Rosskamm, president and CEO of Jo-Ann Stores Inc., growing up in the retail fabric business seemed … ordinary. Looking back, he realizes that his family had to be incredibly nimble in adjusting to changes in the retail market, a realm where survival is predicated on evolution. What children don't always see is that sometimes change doesn't come easily.

"When I was only 10 years old, I started working in my grandmother's store, which was then Cleveland Fabrics, straightening thread racks and folding fabric remnants," Alan recalls. "I guess I had an unusual upbringing because both of my parents worked at the store." Business talk was common at the dinner table; the fabric store has always been part of his life.

Alan worked at the store through high school and college, and watched the business grow from a single storefront to a multi-unit chain. By 1969, it had grown to 169 stores in 28 states and become a publicly held corporation. And it was his father, Martin, who was responsible for much of that change.

"In its earliest days, my dad noticed an emerging trend that instead of stores on a sidewalk or street front, there was a shopping-center movement with room for parking for customers in front of the store," says Alan. "So when the original strip centers were built at Westgate, Southgate, Eastgate, Shoregate and Southland, Cleveland Fabrics opened a store in every one of them."

It was a trend that helped the company grow beyond its Cleveland roots into cities such as Akron, Canton, Youngstown and Pittsburgh. But by the time Alan joined the business in 1978, it was in the midst of another transition. Following a retail trend toward larger, regional malls, his father went back to a smaller store format, and opened 4,000-square-foot stores in those venues.

The evolution was still far from over, however. By 1985, less than seven years later, the company began to encounter difficulties.

"The smaller stores were no longer competitive," says Alan. "They were designed to compete with the department stores who had all gotten out of the [fabric] business. And wherever we looked, there were competitors opening up across from the malls in strip centers in stores that were between 10,000 and 12,000 square feet."

Which meant they could carry larger selections. The company faced the prospect of leaving the malls and heading back to the storefronts.

"The 4,000-square-foot store was being badly out-assorted, but to some degree also undersold because the strip-center rents were cheaper than the mall rents," says Alan.

With performance suffering, and his father getting older, Alan decided to have a conversation with his father. It would change Alan Rosskamm's life and ultimately change the direction of the company.

"I basically told him that I may not be ready, but things are not going that well," Alan says, recalling the bittersweet day he decided to confront his father in his office. "We need to do something and I'd like to try. To his credit, he gave me the chance."

Alan again reinvented the business, moving out of the malls and back into strip

---

JO-ANN STORES INC.
Entrepreneur: Alan Rosskamm
Founded: As Cleveland Fabrics in 1943 by Alan's grandparents Hilda and Berthold Reich, along with their friends Sigmund and Mathilda Rohrbach. The name Jo-Ann Fabrics was derived from the names of the Reich's and the Rohrbach's daughters: Joan Zimmerman and Jacqueline Ann Rosskamm, and was adopted in the mid-'60s. Jacqueline's son Alan was named president and CEO in 1985.
Employees: 20,000-plus

centers, opening larger, 12,000-square-foot stores. He also decided to move in a selection of craft items as a convenience for his customers.

"It was a pretty dramatic change in strategy, and my dad was very supportive," says Alan. "Although he gave me a lot of advice privately, he refrained from publicly criticizing any of the changes I wanted to make. His support was important because he was still chairman of the board. But he was also a great entrepreneur."

The move put the company back on a fast growth track, but there were still hurdles to be cleared. In the early 1990s, retail began to consolidate. It was time to eat or be eaten. So Alan began to look toward competitors to feed Jo-Ann's growth. The largest came in 1994, when the company acquired Clothworld, a 342-store, St. Louis, Mo.-based company with stores throughout the south. At the time of the acquisition, Jo-Ann operated 655 stores, primarily located in the northern United States — so it was a perfect geographic fit.

Responding to yet another change in the retail landscape, the very next year Jo-Ann opened a 46,000-square-foot test store, adjacent to its Cleveland headquarters, stocked with every imaginable creative item to "serve and inspire creativity." The store became the pilot for the new, larger Jo-Ann superstores — what's referred to in retail as a "category killer."

Today, the chain is in the midst of yet another major change, closing its traditional 12,000- to 14,000-square-foot strip-center stores and opening superstores that are 35,000 square feet or larger — stores with product assortments that make them a destination for sewing enthusiasts, stores that offer a full assortment of craft, floral, framing and other home-decorating products. Jo-Ann opened 29 superstores in 2004 and another 40 in 2005, and has commitments for 60 more in 2006.

"I think the biggest accomplishment of my career has been the ability to reinvent our business," says Alan. "If I had stayed in smaller stores in regional malls, we would have never survived. And now, we're reinventing ourselves once again."

So what does the future hold for a company that has emerged as the leading fabric retailer in a fiercely competitive retail market?

"Change," says Alan. "It's almost impossible to look 20 years down the road, but I can predict that our company will be hard to recognize today from whatever it will become 20 years from now. By then it will have evolved and changed into something else."

Who knows? Maybe the next generation will decide to swoop in and shake things up one more time. In a family that refuses to fear change, anything is possible … except defeat.

Jo-Ann Stores Inc.

Johnny Come Profitably

Remember that **wacky invention** you came up with for the seventh-grade science fair? What if you never lost your teenage **belief** in your abilities to create? You might end up like Tony and Mark — successful, profitable, not even 40 yet.

Tony Dellamano, left, and Mark Kuperman outside their store at Parmatown Mall, with the fruits of their labor in hand.

T ony Dellamano and Mark Kuperman met at Cornell University's graduate school in the fall of their first year there. Young and hungry for the business world, their friendship grew and a plan formed.

Mark, through years of working in food service, had developed an idea for an apple snack. He was a food experimenter of sorts, and Applestix were one of his inventions. He knew people liked fruit, and like to snack, so why not battered, fried apple slices? The idea just needed a little refinement and strategy.

Enter Tony. Mark approached his friend with the idea, and the marketing-minded cohort agreed to help turn it into a concept. "We did a lot of development and networking at Cornell," says Mark. "It laid the foundation for our graduation to a true entrepreneurship."

Make that young, hungry and very savvy — they were grad students after all, broke but ambitious. Cornell was the perfect environment. They developed the Johnny Applestix concept basically for free as they navigated grad school, by making it a part of their class projects. For a class in restaurant design, they designed a Johnny Applestix store; for classes in human resources and marketing they used Johnny Applestix as the model.

These guys were testing and tweaking their business plan on somebody else's dime, and getting really good at it.

But it was writing a business plan about Johnny Applestix for a class in entrepreneurship that really got them on the map. They won the school's annual business-plan competition, which gave them credibility and viability in the eyes of Cornell alumni, plus a cool $10,000.

OK, so they had a plan — a winning one at that. Now, simply follow the plan to the letter and success will surely follow. Right?

Well … they only had to modify a couple of very tiny details — location, funding and product. In business, as in life, rule No. 1 is that things don't always go according to plan.

The guys headed to Southern California to make their foodie dream a reality, initially choosing Los Angeles as the location.

"L.A. is a hub for fast food," says Mark. "Plus we had both recently lived in Southern California, so we had a support group and contacts there." They took steps to raise money and find a location, but after securing about half the money they needed, they hit a wall. Getting into the malls there was more difficult than planned. The complexes wouldn't even talk to them as a startup; they didn't want to take the risk of renting to an unknown.

It was a tough six months in Southern California. Tony and Mark were working very hard and getting frustrated that nothing was coming of their efforts. They admit they could have been getting the business started while working full-time jobs, but that would have been too distracting. The security of having a good-paying job would have been hard to give up. "We were working full time on this," says Mark. "There were days when we did everything we could do by 11 a.m. Those were hard, discouraging times."

Tony and Mark began reaching out to their entire network of contacts. One of them was Mark Brandt, a venture capitalist in Cleveland who is also a Cornell alumnus. He knew of Tony and Mark from the business-plan competition. They called to see if Brandt knew of anyone to contact about investing in Johnny Applestix. "He called us back to say he saw an opportunity for us, but we would have to move to Cleveland to do it," says Mark.

Their response? A simple, enthusiastic, "Let's do it." They were passionate about getting the business started and making it work, and here was an invitation — much more appealing than their current tire-spinning out in California. It was a no-brainer. Brandt invited them to town for a presentation to investors, and almost everyone there wrote a check. "And it wasn't just about money," says Mark. "We hooked up with people who could open doors for us."

So Tony, Mark and Johnny Applestix hung up their board shorts, put away their flip-flops and arrived in Cleveland in January 2004. Nothing like a brisk, subzero wind blowing off Lake Erie to get you ready to do business.

Through a good relationship with an investor, they secured a location at Parmatown Mall. They also opened in Jacobs Field in April of that year. "We got a huge amount of PR buzz from that," Mark says. "It gave us credibility with investors and vendors. It really opened things up for us." They think of Johnny Applestix as a Cleveland company, not a transplant, and Jacobs Field emotionally ties them in.

The numbers that first year were not what they expected. "We originally saw ourselves as a sweet-snack company," says Mark. "But now we're seeing ourselves as a fruit-snack company." When the Applestix (battered and fried apple slices served with a range of dipping sauces including vanilla, lemon cheesecake and peanut butter) weren't enough, they added raw Applestix for the health conscious and caramel apples for the traditionalists.

Tony and Mark admit they originally had a pretty rigid view of how to run a business. Since opening, they've learned that flexibility is key. "We often have to take a step back and rethink how to make it work, make the concept better, make people connect with it," says Mark.

The bright-eyed graduate students with a crazy plan for frying apples and selling them to the world are, a decade later, business professionals with experience under their belts. But there's still a little bit of that college-kid excitement left in them — and it's clear that it'll always be there.

JOHNNY APPLESTIX
Entrepreneurs: Tony Dellamano and Mark Kuperman
Founded: Arrived in Cleveland in 2004
Employees: 20

3

ENTREPRENEURIAL

SEIZURE

The Prince and the *(Leveraged-Buyout)* Peas

You're 44 years old, president of
a national company, making the
big bucks and the big decisions.
Think you would ever walk
away from all of that?
Ron Trzcinski did, and lived to tell the tale.

I n August 1989, the president and COO of the Ohio Mattress Company, then the nation's largest mattress retailer, left his dream job. He left a position running a $600-million company that employed more than 5,000 people. He left a title that carried with it an attractive six-figure salary and all the perks that the bigwig corporate heads are used to. And the best part?

He left it to be unemployed.

It wasn't that Ron Trzcinski didn't like his job. He did. Until the leveraged-buyout crew sauntered into town.

"We had a philosophy of how we would do business," he says. "But when you're dealing with these leveraged-buyout guys, cash is king. It's no longer about long-term thinking. They were thinking about their exit strategy before they even bought the company."

And that, to Ron, was simply unacceptable. It was time to leave, to pack up his office and slip out the door. But the buyout men weren't going to let him go quietly into the night.

"When we were interviewed by the potential buyers, I told them I was gone," Ron recalls. "I would be fair and give them a year's notice, but I wasn't staying."

It was a bluff just waiting to be called … or so the buyout guys thought. After all, here was a young, aggressive executive, making a power play at a very key time. It was an intriguing stance — and it marked the kind of man they wanted to keep as their chief executive.

So they came back after they bought the company, offering Ron even more money, wondering what would get his attention. Instead, he told them flat-out: I don't want to work in this environment.

"They couldn't understand me talking about integrity, and I couldn't understand them talking about money. But they kept saying, 'We're going to make you rich,' " says Ron. So he kept telling them the same thing he'd been telling them: I don't want to work in this environment.

"We were both talking, but we couldn't even hear each other," he says. "We were on such a different wavelength."

Ron grew up in Slavic Village, a Southeast Cleveland neighborhood that adhered to that old adage, "It takes a village to raise a child."

"I literally had 200 mothers growing up," he says, "which, looking back on it, was a good thing."

The women instilled a solid value system that remains a vital part of his

Ron Trzcinski goes factory direct, and you can take that to the bank.

character: It influenced his decision to leave the Ohio Mattress Factory without looking back.

And the most important character trait? For Ron, it's integrity. "When I die," he says, "I want my tombstone to say that I was a good guy, not that I made a whole bunch of money."

As a young man, Ron used to help the elderly residents of his neighborhood with their small investments. "They thought I was smart because I went to college," he explains. "For them, just completing high school was a big thing, so I guess it's all relative."

The experience was memorable, especially the day he helped a gentleman who paid him a huge compliment.

"The thing about you is that everybody can trust you," Ron recalls the man telling him. "They can leave all their money on the table and leave, and when they come back, it will all be there."

It was a moment that Ron would carry with him for the rest of his life: A moment that solidified the importance of integrity and signaled the culmination of a good upbringing and a solid work ethic.

That ironclad moral code infuses every square inch of his current business: The Original Mattress Factory.

That's right; the guy who walked away from one mattress company is back on the scene running a new mattress company, on his own terms.

When Ron got bored with an all-play, no-work lifestyle, and realized that he wasn't going to be independently wealthy forever, he started looking at his options.

"I decided that because I knew the business as good as anyone else, I would go into the mattress business," he says.

He had heard about companies that were working a different angle: Going factory-direct to the public, eliminating the middleman and offering big savings to the consumer.

"But it wasn't really something that I had ever thought of," he says. "So you could say I had the knowledge, but didn't have the idea."

When the idea did come to him, it was only a matter of days before Ron worked out his plans in detail. Within a week he was looking at properties.

"Was I afraid of failure? Yes," he admits.

While he had the support of his family and friends, many contemporaries thought the idea simply wouldn't work. The mattress business was driven by brand strength and intense retail promotion. The idea of a store that offered consistently low prices by actually owning the factory and making their own mattresses was novel.

"My wife and kids thought I could do anything," says Ron. "They didn't think this was a big deal. But my friends in the industry said I was nuts. 'You can't sell mattresses that aren't on sale, because the public buys sales,' they said. 'They buy the sizzle, not the steak.'"

But Ron still thought the idea would work.

"I knew we were in a better position to be able to sell a better value, which is quality and low price," he says, "and that's the foundation that built our business. We're definitely proud of our honesty here. We wanted to create a company that was a throwback. A place where people could come in and get value, where we did business in a fair way."

For that reason, Ron teaches

THE ORIGINAL MATTRESS FACTORY
Entrepreneur: Ron Trzcinski
Founded: 1990

salespeople at the Cleveland-based Original Mattress Factory to be courteous and to provide consumers with all the information they need to make a decision. No high-pressure sales or promotions.

"We started with a good idea, but to be successful, you need something to hold that idea together, because times change," he says. "That's where our corporate philosophy comes in.

"I think about it as two values: The values you have from inside, those characteristics we possess that make us who we are, and then the product of value that we offer."

Which has made the Original Mattress Factory a success, and one of the premier brands in the mattress-and-bedding industry.

"Profit and loss is a report card," he says, "a score card, a won-lost record. But I don't sit in the Original Mattress Factory and say, 'How do we make a profit?' I ask, 'How can we do a better job? How can we make people want to come in? How can we make a better bed?' If you do all those things, you will make a profit."

A shrewd businessman to the end, though, Ron is quick to add one caveat: "Those things might make you a real good company, and very successful in your own right," he says, "but it won't make you an Original Mattress Factory."

It's a Small World

The management team at Hanson
Services Inc. hails from all over the globe.
They're a microcosm of old Cleveland
diversity, and this ethnic range is
contributing to an *old-world* idea:
Treat your elders with respect.
Mary Ann Hanson is out to prove that
you can build a *successful* company by
caring about your community.

Mary Ann Hanson focuses on creating an atmosphere of respect in every aspect of her business.

"We speak 14 languages here," says Hanson Services Inc. founder and President Mary Ann Hanson.

There's the CFO from Nepal and his Romanian assistant. They work not far from the Ukrainian manager of information systems, who sits a stone's throw from the caregiver coordinator from Belarus. Then there's Michael Abraham, Mary Ann's husband and the company's chief of operations. Of Portuguese descent, he was born in Macao and came to America by way of Hong Kong.

One of Mary Ann's first employees was Moldovan. And don't forget the Russian she hired as a personal assistant. She had only one complaint about her new hometown: too wet. "In Siberia, where it was 50 degrees colder, at least it was dry," says Mary Ann.

We almost hesitate to mention the social worker from England. He, after all, only speaks English.

Mary Ann refers to her latest endeavor as "my retirement project gone awry" — she started Hanson Services at the age of 54.

　　　　　　　　　　　　　　　　　　　　Hanson Services Inc.

"I put together a nifty business plan," she says. "The bankers were intrigued, but didn't think it would work."

"It" was the concept of providing all the nonmedical services — laundry and housekeeping, meal planning and preparation, pet and plant care and whatever else — to enable senior citizens to continue living in their own homes, on their own terms.

Undeterred by head-scratching bankers, she started Hanson Services without money or clients, just confidence in herself and a deep respect for the people she'd serve and hire. She sat down at her kitchen table and wrote her first brochure.

Mary Ann is a bubbly woman full of stories and humorous anecdotes. When you see her life in review, it seems inevitable that she'd end up doing exactly what she's doing.

Her father died in an accident when she was 2, and her mother was often away working as a nurse at a small hospital. Her uncle was a physician, as was her first husband.

At the age of 12, she was probably mistakenly diagnosed with rheumatic fever, and she spent the next six months in a hospital. "I had my own private room and I rode through the halls in a dirty-laundry cart," she remembers, and she loved every minute of it.

When not flying down hospital corridors, she lived much of the time with her grandparents.

"I never thought of them as old," she says of the couple universally known as Uncle Mack and Aunt Molly.

Admittedly, that universe was rather small. The couple owned a grocery store that served the farmers near the town of Alzey, Ky., population three.

"Just my grandfather, my grandmother and me. That was the entire town."

From them, Mary Ann learned the importance of cash-flow management and developed her entrepreneurial bent. But beyond that, she grew up learning and thriving on the strength and knowledge of loving caregivers who were well into their "golden years."

She spent most of her career in the health care field, and in 1991 assumed management of the Normandy apartments, a 157-unit complex in Rocky River whose residents' average age was 87. There, she found a situation she refers to as "caregivers gone wild." Many of the residents had been cajoled into paying an hourly rate for assistance from unlicensed freelance caregivers who were also billing as many as nine or 10 other residents for their services at the same time.

"The first thing I did was institute quality controls," she says. She got rid of the unlicensed caregivers and hired a more dependable, responsive crew.

By 1995, Mary Ann was disillusioned. Her last few jobs involved working with an elderly population, and she didn't like what she'd seen — she was looking for something that could effectively help the seniors she encountered.

She knew there were many seniors who needed assistance but didn't want to leave their homes, and why should they? As long as they received a level of individualized non-medical assistance that matched their needs, whether for a few hours a couple times a week or for 36 hours — her clients' weekly average — there was no reason why they couldn't remain at home as long as they were medically able to do so.

"In a facility, you're buying an hour and a half a day of hands-on care," says Mary Ann. "In your home, you're going to have a solid one-on-one for four hours a day — or however long you need it."

It was the beginning of Hanson Services.

Mary Ann went to The Alzheimer's Association with her homemade brochure and came away with almost more work than she could handle.

"At first, it was one desk, one computer," recalls Kanchan Adhikary, the company's chief financial officer. "Then we actually got assigned desks."

By 2005, projected billing had risen to $6 million. Hanson Services now has multiple offices in Ohio and Florida, and has made the Weatherhead 100 (which tracks the fastest-growing companies in Northeast Ohio) twice. One year the company was named the eighth-fastest-growing privately held company in the region and the following year it was ranked 22nd.

So where did she find the kind of caregivers she required? Right here in Cleveland, sort of.

"Eastern Europeans reserve their deepest respect for the most elderly members of their families," she says. "If an 18-year-old girl has a problem, she's going to go to her grandmother." So in her quest for good employees, Mary Ann went after immigrants as much as the Americans born and raised here.

One of her first employees at the Normandy apartment complex was a former surgical ophthalmology nurse from Moldova who spoke virtually no English.

"I don't know how we got through the interview, but there was a lot of smiling

HANSON SERVICES INC.
Entrepreneur: Mary Ann Hanson
Founded: 1996
Employees: More than 300

and nodding," Mary Ann recalls. "She was so wonderful that the residents adopted her and taught her English."

Mary Ann was also able to find a more educated work force among the new arrivals. Her self-taught MIS director was a psychiatrist in Ukraine who went back to school to learn about computers.

Veslava Pikous came to Cleveland to escape the political situation in her native Belarus, where she and her husband owned a trucking firm. "I love it here. It's a great team," she says. "We're free to do whatever we think is right for the company. Whatever it takes to bring us up, up, up, and to be the best, which we are."

To many of Mary Ann's immigrant staffers that sense of freedom is as foreign as their new homeland. "Eastern Europeans worked under politicos," she says. "Their biggest fear was making mistakes because they were afraid of getting caught and being ostracized and belittled. Some would deny making errors until they saw that they weren't going to get in trouble for it."

Mary Ann may not have changed the whole world with her "retirement project," but she has created a model company based on a revolutionary principle: respect. The secret, she's learned, is to go with the flow. One client, for instance, would repeatedly make the clean laundry disappear. After a long search, Hanson found the clothing under the woman's mattress. She put it in its proper place, but found it once again in its odd storage place.

"After that," she says with a shrug and a smile, "I put the clean laundry under the mattress."

Thinking *Inside* the Box

Clinton Morgan was lucky
enough to see his **career path**
sitting right in front of him,
gathering dust.
But, as with any successful business,
it was hard work and **foresight**,
not luck, that got Clinton where
he is today.

You might say Clinton Morgan was an early bloomer. By the tender age of 8, the budding businessman had already started his first business: picking and selling blackberries by the quart. By 11, he moved into a different facet of consumer goods: digging up and selling worms to fishermen. To supplement his independent endeavors, he worked on paper routes and in bicycle repair shops.

The little boy from Georgia had big plans, and when he got to college he found a professor who helped him home in on his future.

Clinton's economic teacher at Johnson C. Smith University in Charlotte, N.C., continuously encouraged students to own their own businesses. "He used to pound into our heads that there were not enough black manufacturers around," Clinton remembers. "That always stuck with me."

After graduation, Clinton studied for his MBA at New York University and worked summers as a recreation leader for the city of New York in the Bureau of Child Welfare. "That job was just about being able to make money to go to school," Morgan says. In the back of his mind, he continued to hear his econ professor's words.

Eventually, Clinton's career path aligned with Cleveland: In a serendipitous twist, he was transferred here by Westvaco, the paper manufacturing company he was working for as a sales representative. The timing turned out to be crucial.

"This is where it all starts for me," he says.

During his time with Westvaco in Cleveland, Clinton went through two union strikes. Both times, the sales reps were pulled in to work in the plant and cover for the striking workers.

"I gained some hands-on experience I would never regret," he notes.

But it was the strike in 1976 that really gave Clinton an idea. "This time when I was working at the plant, I paid very close attention to what I was doing," he says. He noticed equipment sitting on the sidelines of the factory. The retired machines had been used to make the types of corrugated cardboard products Clinton sold.

That type of cardboard was a specialty product, not the kind of thing the big companies wanted to be doing anymore — it was cumbersome and costly to produce. Clinton saw that the customers were still using it, even if producers didn't care to supply it. Westvaco ended most mass production of the product and relegated what was left to a lone plant in Sandusky. It wasn't attempting to build demand for the product or even retain its current customers.

Clinton saw an opportunity. "I decided I could use it as a base to start a company

MORGAN PACKAGING
Entrepreneur: Clinton Morgan
Founded: 1976
Employees: 10

Starting with little more than an idea and some used equipment, Clinton Morgan capitalized on a niche market.

of my own," he says.

Combine rejected business with mothballed machines and *voila!* You've got yourself an untapped niche market. Or so Clinton thought.

It was a notable idea, but not an original one. At that time, around 1976, there were six to eight companies that started this type of marketing in the area. "They all saw the same opportunity," Clinton says. In fact, most of them were salesmen from the large companies, just like him.

But his charm and people skills had provided solid business relationships, so he had a leg up in the business with an existing client base. He created a winning business plan and networked even more, eventually finding investors who believed in him.

Clinton put his manufacturing plant together gradually. He started looking for a building, bought some of the Westvaco equipment and went to a used machinery market for additional pieces. "In the very beginning," he says, "it was just me and two employees. I did everything — operated machines, opened mail, answered phones. Everything."

Morgan Packaging became known as a sheet plant, able to manufacture in small quantities instead of just bulk orders like some of the larger companies. It was able to make one box or 1,000 boxes. Its specialty became custom orders, the type of business the larger companies were no longer interested in.

Recently, box-making has morphed — and once again, large national companies are starting to fill smaller, custom orders. The niche is making a comeback.

"Now those larger companies are putting a lot of emphasis on what we've been doing, and the competition is fierce," Clinton says.

Luckily Clinton has been in this niche market longer, so he has an advantage, right? Not exactly. "There are no advantages," he says. "There have never been any advantages in this business. It's always about competition." Clinton is faithful that his long-standing customers will see him through, and that his business savvy and people skills will continue to generate business for Morgan Packaging.

But the competition can be especially tough for minority business owners. "It's a twofold challenge," says Clinton. "You're always under a microscope, whether you're not getting business because you're a minority or you are getting business but you have to beat a competitor on product, service or price."

There is also an obligation to the community at large and to the minority business community. "There is a feeling of alignment among minority entrepreneurs," he notes, "because in reality we're all in the same boat. We have to support each other as much as possible.

"Someone will always be there to tell you how hard it is to start a new business, and how crazy you are to attempt it, but," says Clinton, "you have to follow your dream." And make your economics teacher proud.

This *Little* Polymer Went to Market ...

So this little old lady in Cleveland kept jabbering about some **invention** that would change how we **conduct heat.** Who knew she wasn't little, old or in the mood to get beaten down by the naysayers? **Welcome** to Carol Latham's version of David and Goliath.

Scientist Carol Latham had a late-1980s polymer problem. That is to say, she was deep in the midst of traditional research at oil giant British Petroleum and she and her polymer were bumping into the lingering glass ceiling in her field.

She was a part of BP's idea-development team, a cohort that supported the various businesses BP was acquiring. It focused on solving industrial problems, and for Carol that meant designing ceramic substrates (heat conductors) for electronics. Heat conduction in the new, smaller electronic devices entering the market was becoming a bigger problem — one that many companies wanted to be the first to solve.

But Carol realized something during her research: Ceramics weren't the answer to the question. The substrates could conduct heat, but they were bulky and inflexible. The idea fueled her interest in polymers, a type of plastic. She began working to develop a better way to conduct heat using the soft, formable polymers instead of hard, brittle ceramics, and crafted a proposal to do a project based on her research.

"Of course it fell between the cracks a number of times," she says, "but I was eventually able to bring it to the forefront." Falling between the cracks was a common problem for Carol's work. Because she was a woman in a man's field? Perhaps. But for Carol, the bottom line was that she wasn't moving forward. The delay just meant one thing: frustration.

"Finally, the men said, 'Maybe she'll be quiet for a while if we let her do this,' " Carol remembers. She began her research, and got results that were unexpected. Better than she had ever thought they would be. Ultimately, she did discover a new way to conduct heat — her polymer idea worked. It was a discovery that would revolutionize the way electronics are made. But the huge corporation she worked for wasn't paying attention.

So Carol took her little polymer and left BP. Surely, she thought, she would find backers ready and willing to take her product to market. Her definition of an entrepreneur? Someone who starts a business without any product, customers, employees, offices or money. "Just me and my vision. That's it," she says. "I really was naïve."

Carol wrote a business plan, believing that investors would sign up quickly.

"From the little bit that I had been around, I thought that if you could demonstrate a product that there was a need for, getting money would not be such a big deal,"

Carol Latham never meant to be an inventor, but her time in the lab has been well spent.

she says. "That there would be people out there that would want to back you."

But that was a matter of timing. In the early '80s, venture capital was big and available, but by the early '90s, it had fallen flat. She wrote letters to venture capitalists all over the country, getting nowhere. "I could get interest from people in Silicon Valley who understood what it was about, but they didn't want to invest in some company in Cleveland, Ohio," she says. "I think they thought, doubtfully, 'There's some little old lady in Cleveland saying she can move heat.' " Carol wasn't moving to California — her home was here, as were family and friends. So she continued the uphill trudge.

Carol went for two and a half years without an income. She rented out her house in Lakewood, moved into an apartment in Mentor and rented a little corner of production space in which she could fully develop her polymer-based conductor.

Finally, she had a breakthrough. Carol found an attorney who drafted a private placement letter, allowing her to legally take money from individuals. She would be able to offer shares of stock to interested investors.

"I did have one stipulation," she says. "I wouldn't borrow money from my friends, because that sort of thing ruins relationships." So she targeted friends of friends, the next tier out, people she knew in the community who had a little extra money for a good cause. Initially, she enlisted five shareholders. "They said, 'If she is willing to put her whole self and her life on the line for this, she must really have something.' " And they were right. Thermagon Inc. was born.

In 1992, within a few months of getting the money ($70,000 to start), Carol hired two people. That year, sales were $70,000. In 1994 the company broke even and by the following year sales were doubling. Its biggest dilemma was that it didn't have a travel or advertising budget, but also didn't have customers in Cleveland. So Carol worked very hard to get new product releases in technical journals, then followed up avidly with anyone who responded. She sent them free samples of her product, saying, "Don't believe me, but this is what our material can do. Test it." The little polymer started to generate interest in Silicon Valley.

But the biggest step forward for Thermagon came in 1995, when Carol got a call from Intel Corp. It wanted to take Carol's polymer all the way to Asia. The rest is Thermagon history. Carol hurriedly found an agent in Taiwan to act as her representative. That agent has turned out to be one of Carol's closest business associates over the years, and Intel signed on to use the product in its Pentium chips. "We got a lot of business through that deal," she says. "But mostly it gave me something I had been missing all those years: credibility." It seemed the whole world had finally discovered Thermagon.

That was the beginning. Thermagon grew fourfold the next year and kept growing until the downturn of 2001. Through all of it, Carol received offers to buy the company. But she wasn't ready to sell … until recently.

"I have put my whole life into this, and I'm not getting any younger," she says. "Now I think it's time." But it had to be to the right company. She sold not to a Fortune 500 company, but to mid-sized Laird Technologies, a company based out of St. Louis. Thermagon will stay in Cleveland, and Carol plans to stay on with Laird as global product director until she's ready to leave.

So what's next? Certainly not retirement. "My next project is to get involved in inspiring others to follow their dreams and do what they want to," Carol says. She's still driven by wanting to find the answers. "I'm a techno geek," she admits. "I'm interested in how technology can solve the world's problems. And now I know a thing or two about getting it to market."

THERMAGON INC.
Entrepreneur: Carol Latham
Founded: 1991
Employees: 95

4

IT STUCK

TO THE WALL

You Say *Potato,* I Say *Broccoli*

Some people play it **safe**, following
the rule book to moderate success.
A few are **born** under a lucky star.
But every once in a while, you meet
a man who follows a **different** path:
He says yes when others say no,
turns daydreams into **reality**,
climbs to the top because he
knows he can.

G lazen Creative Studios is everything you'd expect from a high-tech video-production company. Smart, stylish and progressive, it strikes a comfortable balance between slick and substantive. It's the best in the business — *the* place companies come to when they need video. It all comes from approaching the industry a little differently.

Founder Alan Glazen doesn't keep time logs. He doesn't judge his producers on profitability. Employees are never told how many hours they should spend on a project, what tools to use or how many days are allowed for shooting. And in his mind, it's the only way to stay on top.

"That's our business formula: Do whatever it takes to produce excellence and feel proud," says Glazen. "If it's excellent, we're confident that we'll come out on top." And the company does, consistently. Its account list reads like the blue book of Cleveland industry: Sherwin-Williams, American Greetings, KeyCorp, National City.

In 1972, just out of college, Alan was already itching to get off the beaten path. Instead of taking his creative brainpower to someone else's company, he decided to break out on his own, starting an ad agency with $80 to his name. It was first called Opinion Concepts Inc. Once it seemed destined for success it was renamed Glazen Advertising.

Alan's first client was Cook Coffee Co., which owned Uncle Bill's Discount Stores. Cook liked the work he did and began referring him to other companies it owned. At the same time, political candidates hired him and referred him to others in the Democratic party.

Through sheer tenacity — outworking the next guy and not sleeping much — the agency went on through the years to become a $30 million company that won an extraordinary number of industry awards, including induction into the Cleveland Advertising Hall of Fame for Alan. In fact, in 1987 Glazen swept the Cleveland Addys, winning awards that, Alan points out, didn't even really make sense, like best art direction for a radio commercial. "We were winning a lot of recognition for our broadcast work," he says.

It continued like that for a few more years. But 1991 began to see significant changes in the Cleveland ad industry. Mid-sized agencies were being threatened by huge, regional agencies that could be the be-all end-all for advertising needs. So Glazen decided to go in the opposite direction. After all, it had never been Alan's

Masters of their own creativity, from left: Glazen Creative Studios founder Alan Glazen and partners Ron Goldfarb and Tony Weber.

intention to go along with standard procedure or proven methods. He wanted Glazen to be a standout company producing unheard-of results, and he knew it would take guts, quick thinking and a very open mind to achieve it. An over-the-top mission? Perhaps, but all the more enticing for its improbability.

Alan asked himself, "What if we could be a center of excellence to be available to [clients] just when they needed it?" Glazen's center of excellence was producing video. "The big companies knew and respected our name and always valued us pertaining to television," he says.

It took nerve to rebrand the company. Glazen was perceived as an ad agency, not as a production company: It was the design aspect of Alan's business that had helped build his reputation. But Glazen was actually the only agency around writing, producing, directing and editing its own commercials.

At the time, Alan had a competitor who inadvertently inspired him to go into this niche of the business. He saw his competitor gathering tons of work producing industrial videos, and realized there was a huge gap in the creativity between the art in commercials and the art in business videos. He figured he could do it better than the rest of the field. "I decided it was time to bring our kind of artistry into that kind of work," he says.

Alan changed the company's name to Glazen Creative Group, then to Glazen Creative Studios, and reopened shop as a hybrid communication department with the front end of an ad agency and the back end of a real production company. "Unlike a typical video studio where you have basically an editor and a shooter, we came with decades of deep knowledge of how marketing works," says Alan. Never before in Cleveland had all this been available from one company.

Alan calls his next move the most clever of his life. He identified the two best people at his competitor's firm, Tony Weber and Ron Goldfarb. In 2002, he wooed them over to Glazen and made them his partners. For Glazen Creative Studios, the world changed. It turned out they were more right than they thought. "The companies really took to us, to the idea of what we could do," Alan says. "Now companies could come in to talk about their communications strategy first instead of coming in to simply say 'make me a video.'"

"Certainly, Tony and Ron were both scared to come over here," he continues. "It was a big risk for all of us." One that paid off, big time.

The company's reputation for excellence at any cost has gotten around. Today, when there's an important project in the community, Glazen is always called to the table. "If we want the job, we'll get the job," says Ron. In fact, according to Ron, when the Cleveland Museum of Art needed a video solution to rally support for its expansion, Glazen was the only company it talked to. It's one of the company's favorite projects, as are most of the nonprofit projects it takes on.

"Nonprofit work is always win-win," says Alan. Glazen produces it at a reduced cost, which helps the organization it's working with, but the trade-off is that the work allows for creative freedom — no strict list of objectives, just the goal of telling a compelling story. When Glazen received the Smart Business Network's Pillar Award in 2001 for its community service, the company thanked its corporate clients for funding the ability to do nonprofit work.

GLAZEN CREATIVE STUDIOS
Entrepreneur: Alan Glazen
Founded: Alan started Opinion Concepts Inc. in 1972, which evolved into his current business during the '90s.
Employees: 11

Because Alan removes traditional hurdles, the Glazen staff is able to be at its most creative; the results are stunning. "It's unbelievable how many of our clients get teary when we show them the final piece. Then we know it's a home run," he says. One of its most well-received pieces was a heartfelt company-culture video commissioned by The Sherwin-Williams Co. as part of a contest application to *Fortune* magazine. Guess what? It worked, earning Sherwin-Williams a spot on *Fortune*'s list of the 100 best companies to work for. And earning Glazen Creative another one of those moments.

"All we ask is that our employees make our clients ecstatic," says Alan. And the company keeps it fresh with what it calls an amazing, almost outrageous devotion to knocking clients out. "Everybody here wants that moment — wants clients to be bowled over."

Turning on the Charm

When Packy Hyland Jr. **founded** Hyland Software, he assembled a crack **team** of professionals with experience in software architecture, business operations and finance. The only thing he didn't have was **money.**

It might not take a village to start a successful company without venture capital, but it does take some good people. Packy Hyland Jr. had those in spades in 1991, when Hyland Software Inc. was just a dream.

The company evolved from a small computer-networking business Packy Jr. started with his dad's help. Recognizing a need for innovative technology based on customer and market needs, Packy started gathering people and his father began looking for money.

"Those were amazing times," says Packy's younger brother, A.J. Hyland, now president and CEO of the organization described by *Inc.* magazine as one of the fastest-growing privately held companies in the nation. "I credit a lot of it to my dad. He could get money out of a rock."

Packy Jr.'s skills came in handy, too. A natural entrepreneur and charismatic leader, but also quirky, spontaneous and abrupt, Packy Jr. knew exactly what he wanted.

"Each of us had a set of skills that brought something to the table, something that represented another piece of the puzzle," says A.J. "There were times that were tense, but everyone was rowing in the same direction, pulling on their own oar any way they could. And it all worked out."

Engineers Miguel and Alfonso Zubizarreta, brothers the Hylands met through the original computer-networking business, became Packy's designers. Packy and A.J.'s brother Chris Hyland was brought in to handle the money. Packy's friend Bill Priemer was in charge of operations.

Meanwhile, a crucial part of the team was ... still in college.

"Even then, Packy was putting the hard press on me," says A.J. of his older brother. "He wanted me to quit college and just start working. But I wanted to finish and get my degree. I told him I'd join the company when I finished school, and he was comical about it."

But A.J. did start working with Hyland Software while still in school, testing software programs and protocol using his school computer — much to the consternation of his college roommates at Georgetown. Despite having no formal training in software development, he had a natural grasp of the functions the software designers were trying to create.

"I would test the software in my days off and then fax my problems and concerns back to Miguel. His development team would work on the corrections and I would retest the software to make sure everything was fixed," says A.J. "But I had a 96-baud modem and was downloading from DOS-based Bulletin Board System in the

A.J. Hyland was a college kid with an older brother who had a plan for a business; today he's the president of the company.

days prior to the Internet. I guess my roommates were upset because I was tying up the phone lines a little too much."

When he finally graduated in '94, A.J. joined the company, which was still struggling through its infancy.

At times during the company's first few years, payroll was met only days before it was due. There was a time in '95 when the major players went without a paycheck.

Attacking the capital-intensive software market without venture capital, or, more importantly, customers, was difficult. While Packy was able to get the organization up and running, it's A.J. who eventually built Hyland's customer base.

"The first thing we needed was customers, and that meant doing some loss leaders," says A.J. "There's nothing worse than going into a sales situation and telling the prospect that you don't have anyone using your product. So I decided to get people on board any way I could, even if it meant giving the software away, and then leveraging those customers."

But giving product away, while a good way to build customers, wasn't the best way to build cash flow.

"Everyone took it on the chin then," says A.J. "Everyone decided to take a pay cut for that six-month period. And we didn't promise anyone that we would be able to pay anyone back. But as credit to my brother, when we started to turn a profit, he calculated how much money it would have been and found a way to pay them back.

"That kind of attitude, and it's the attitude that permeates this company to this day, is something that struck the whole company that we were serious," A.J. points out. "That it wasn't just the Hylands and the Zubizarretas running the place. That this was a place where people could come and truly be a part of something special."

In 1997, Packy made his little brother president of Hyland Software. That's when things really started to click. Customers were discovering their products such as OnBase, a program that helps companies digitize their paper documents into an electronic format. Their software was in use at major financial institutions and the company was able to grow into new markets and in new directions. The next year, the company saw its first profit.

"I remember because we actually had a little party to celebrate our first profitable quarter," says A.J. "And we did it without venture capital. Those first few years were tough, but we made it through."

With the business finally in the black, Packy Jr. got bored. He devised one last shake-up, a real doozie. While on vacation in New England, A.J. got a call.

He figured something had blown up while he was away. Instead, it was Packy, who informed him of his decision to retire and hand the reins over to A.J. He would give his two weeks' notice at the staff meeting the following Monday. Very Packy.

A.J. took the call in stride.

He brought a different set of abilities to the position, traits that have buoyed the company's growth.

"I think it's a mistake to try and be the same kind of personality as your predecessor," Hyland says. "Bring your unique talents to the table, but don't stray from what made the business great. That's why we have our core values listed. As long as those pillars are in place, it doesn't necessarily matter what kind of personality runs the company."

Throughout the transitions, the growth spurts and the lean times, the company has never lost sight of its roots as a tiny father-and-son organization fighting against software giants. The Zubizarretas, brother Chris and buddy Bill Premier are still a part of Hyland Software, which has ballooned to employ more than 460 people. OnBase is recognized as one of the premier software-management solution packages on the market. The tiny team has become something of a giant.

"When my wife comes here today, she can't even recognize the place," says A.J. "From what it was when I joined just over 10 years ago to what it has become today, it's like night and day."

For that matter, neither can A.J., who still credits his brother as the true entrepreneur; and while it was Packy who launched the company, it's A.J. carrying the ball.

"Running a business is a lot like being a running back," he says. "You have to pick your hole and then hit it. Once you get into the defensive backfield, you can start going left and right. You'll know how to get to the end zone."

> HYLAND SOFTWARE INC.
> **Entrepreneur:** A.J. Hyland
> **Founded:** In 1991, by Packy Hyland Jr. His brother A.J. took over in 2001.
> **Employees:** 460-plus

How D'ya Market a Sausage?

There are certainly **easier** things
to sell than ground meat encased in …
that stuff they encase sausages in.
Today, after more than **30 years** in
the biz, the Heinles are pros when
it comes to pushing their product.
How did they do it?
A little pina colada mix, a few mugs
of beer and the **magic** number eight.

It's not the first thing most kids dream about doing when they grow up. Norm Heinle planned on doing the suit-and-tie thing — he graduated from John Carroll University with a degree in business administration. His wife Carol was happy as a registered nurse.

But Kirchberger Sausage had always been there in the background, a part of their old-world Brooklyn, Ohio, neighborhood since 1938. Hans and Elly Kirchberger processed their knackwurst, liverwurst, tongue and pork links themselves, and when Norm was 13 he started helping out around the store.

The aging Kirchbergers liked Norm. By 1968, Carol was raising kids and nursing, Norm was working a very full-time schedule that included classes at JCU and Hans Kirchberger was having a heart attack. Nothing serious as far as those things go, but enough to remind the old immigrant that he and his wife had no succession plan, their own kids grown and uninterested.

And they liked Norm.

So, over a 30-year period, the Kirchbergers slowly transferred the business over to the Heinles. And that's where things started to get interesting.

Carol had to leave nursing. She found herself too busy with child rearing and helping out at the store, which they renamed The Sausage Shoppe in 1979. She has a head for figures, for advertising the business — despite a more low-key personality than her husband's — and for technology. Carol's the detail person, as you can tell by their shared conversations. Norm throws out a date and she flips through documentation before gently correcting him.

But the arena they excel in is "sausage promotion."

The Heinles have run events with local print and broadcast celebs including Joel Crea, Del Donahoo and Neil Zurcker, and been on The Food Network's "Extreme Cuisine."

Their most successful campaign was their own catchy "Eight for Eight for Eight" promotion. "Eight brats on eight buns for eight bucks," chime the Heinles together. It won an award for innovation from the American Society of Meat Processors and the American Pork Producers Council. More importantly, "it made our summer," says Carol.

They developed their famous All-Star brats in the 1980s. Norm explains, "We put mustard and beer in the brats, and it worked so well we're still selling them for Father's Day."

Not that every Sausage Shoppe marketing endeavor has been a home run. The city of Cleveland once produced a video in an ill-fated attempt to draw local hero

Norm and Carol Heinle, flanked by son Allen and daughter Renee, know a lot about making and marketing a sausage.

Drew Carey for some forgotten event. As part of the pitch, the Heinles came up with the Buzz Beer Brat, a beer-and-coffee concoction based on the Buzz Beer the characters drank on Carey's TV show.

"That was one of the worst-tasting things we ever had on the face of the Earth," recalls Norm with a laugh.

Nearly as bad was the "Extreme Cuisine" concept. "We were asked to come up with all these weird flavors of brats," says Norm. "Chocolate chips, strawberries, pina colada ..."

But the challenge of concocting new sausage flavors pales next to the challenge of keeping up in the 21st century. Consumers no longer visit the butcher, the baker and the candlestick maker. They just go to the big-box store.

"Our business is all about surviving in a Wal-Mart world," Norm admits.

They've found success by offering service with a personal touch. "We have one 40-year customer who comes back here from Florida and shows us snapshots of his grandchildren," says Carol.

Then there's the sausage-lover who spent an anxious long weekend until he could show up when the shop reopened to return the $10 bill he'd accidentally been overpaid in change.

And they aren't afraid to admit they don't know it all. The Heinles took courses at the Culinary Institute of America and have attended numerous college seminars and workshops to learn the latest methods and cultural trends. But we live in Cleveland …

"Sometimes we learned too far ahead of the curve," says Carol.

For instance, when they heard of the dangers of cholesterol at the University of Wisconsin in 1990, they came up with heart-friendly cuts that their customers hated.

Same thing when they tried to accept credit cards way before the supermarkets. "It was a flop," says Norm.

Okay, so there have been a few obstacles along the way. But the Heinles found a way over most.

Dennis, their youngest son and now a network administrator in Missouri, put the family business on the Internet — back in 1990. "People in the industry said, 'What are you people doing on the computer? You make meat,' " Norm recalls.

While the Heinles can't ship out of state because they're not federally inspected, they take online orders for pickup by returning emigrants. And Carol has learned about online marketing. She surveys her electronic subscribers for recipes, which she adds to the Web site.

"This is the 2010 woman here," says Norm of his tech-savvy wife.

It's not an easy life: the hours, the competition, the need to meet fickle tastes and changing health guidelines. (One customer told Carol that his doctor ordered him away from all lunch meat "unless you get that lean, preservative-free pork from that sausage place.") But Norm and Carol Heinle have spent their lives together, sharing one small, cramped backroom office when they have the luxury of sitting. Their four kids have worked side by side with them and were sent to top schools; today two of their children help run the business.

THE SAUSAGE SHOPPE
Entrepreneurs: Norm and Carol Heinle
Founded: By Hans and Elly Kirchberger in 1938 as Kirchberger's Sausage. Norm and Carol Heinle began to take over the store in the late '60s and changed the name in 1979.
Employees: 5

The Heinles may not have slain any giants, but they have held their own against the Mike Tysons of the industry.

"It's packaged in Bentonville, Arkansas, it came in from South Dakota, it was shipped within seven days, and you have seven more days to eat it," says Norm of the competition. "Ours was made last night and we're selling it today."

Old Man Kirchberger would be proud.

Relative Success

Sports lovers of the world,
meet your latest heroes:
a few guys from Cleveland Heights
who combined their passion
for sports with a *risky* but
shrewd business plan that's
paying off big time.

The office that Home Team Marketing calls home isn't much more than utilitarian. It's in a looming, century-old former bank building on East 105th Street that looks like it's been only partially tamed through rehabilitation. The HTM suite has a lobby, a handful of private offices and a break room. Nothing to write home about, and yet …

It's heaven, all 1,400 square feet of it, or that's how it must seem. After all, the young guys who run the company started Home Team Marketing four years ago in the attic of the Fitzpatrick family home in Cleveland Heights.

"They spent most of their time in this one maybe 9-by-12 bedroom with a little window air conditioner in the summer," recalls Queenie Fitzpatrick, otherwise known as "Mom" to three of the founders.

Patrick Spear, 26, the only member of the team who's not part of the family, succinctly describes it this way: "There were four of us, one phone, one fax, one computer."

The only time there was any breathing room was if someone was out pitching business. Which didn't happen often. As company President Peter Fitzpatrick, 33, points out, "No one was returning our phone calls, so we had no place to go."

It's fortunate the guys got along so well, but that was pretty much a given. The Fitzpatricks and the Spears grew up together, went to the same schools and lived within a couple blocks of each other in Cleveland Heights. The Fitzpatrick clan includes five boys, and the Spears have four boys and two girls, all with overlapping ages.

"For every Spear there's a Fitzpatrick," says Patrick. "Jake [Fitzpatrick, another partner in the business] was in the hospital room when my mom was having me."

Sport was king. They all played varsity football at powerhouse St. Ignatius High School, Peter ran track, and Patrick was on the basketball team. Peter went on to play running back at Cornell University, and Regan Fitzpatrick (the fourth partner) was a Division III All-American defensive back at Ohio Wesleyan. Before heading off to corporate America, Peter coached for a year at his old high school, where brother Rory is an assistant athletic director.

Peter says his entrepreneurial drive was shared by various Spear brothers through the years. Peter and Brian, a Spear brother close to his age, opened a short-lived frozen French toast business as kids.

"We cooked the French toast the night before and froze it, then sold them after

From left, Regan, Peter and Jake Fitzpatrick and Patrick Spear have come a long way from their attic digs.

Mass that Sunday morning," he says. "But it was harder than we thought, and we got out of the business after one day."

Long before Home Team Marketing won a year's free rent in its current space as part of the $50,000 prize package for its first-place finish in the Council of Smaller Enterprises Business Plan Challenge 2002 — and even longer before they were to establish satellite offices in Cincinnati, Dallas and Seattle — Home Team Marketing started as a round of "what ifs" between Peter and his now 31-year-old brother, Regan.

Both had found jobs after college in large New York advertising agencies, handling accounts that generated business by amply funding professional sports opportunities.

"Peter and I were both buying sponsorship packages from these big leagues that don't need the money, and yet all of these high school programs were in dire need," says Regan.

Which got them thinking: What if they could attract major national and regional advertisers on behalf of high school sports teams starved for funding? They'd seen programs where budgets were squeezed, where kids had to pay to play, and where, year after year, failed levies brought serious discussions about canceling teams altogether.

They could raise money by selling ads in programs and on scoreboards and banners and ticket backs and wherever else schools would permit. Much like what the well-meaning team boosters do on a catch-as-catch-can basis, where efforts are largely confined to the approachable local pizza parlors, funeral homes and the like.

Peter and Regan could focus on the deep-pocketed corporate advertisers. Through the company they envisioned, corporations could make network buys, getting ad placement before spectators at the sporting events of dozens, hundreds or even thousands of schools through a single, knowledgeable contact. Put together large enough networks and they could offer advertisers audience numbers that would dwarf the attendance at most professional sporting events. The Fitzpatricks would take a cut and send much-needed checks to the schools.

Regan got serious about it first. He moved back home and took up office quarters in Queenie and Tim Fitzpatrick's attic. Soon, Peter and his wife quit good jobs and returned to Northeast Ohio. Then the two convinced younger brother Jake, 27, and Patrick to join up.

Now that they had what they optimistically referred to as their "world headquarters," all they had to do was pitch their ingenious concept. How hard could that be?

"I'd get so mad for them when they thought they had something and then it fell through," says Queenie. "I can remember saying to my husband, 'This is the downside of having them here. If they were in an office, I wouldn't be living and dying with them.' "

It was a two-prong sale. HTM had to convince school systems to let the company represent them, and almost simultaneously they had to pique the interest of advertisers. School districts had never seen such a concept and were naturally hesitant to turn over their sports advertising properties to strangers who had no buyers lined up. And with no school systems in hand, HTM had nothing concrete to sell advertisers. They had to explain a concept that only existed in a theoretical sense, admitting to whomever they reached on that single upstairs phone line that if they wanted to see Home Team's track record,

HOME TEAM MARKETING
Entrepreneurs: Brothers Peter, Jake and Regan Fitzpatrick, and family friend Patrick Spear
Founded: 2001
Employees: 14 full time, plus 2-4 part time

they'd have to first sign up and then look in the mirror.

No advertisers. No inventory. No real office, even. Just their stuffy upstairs digs and their "boardroom" for meeting with clients — the family dining room.

Queenie laughs about the time her boys were being interviewed at the dining-room table by an actual business reporter. "I stuck my head in the doorway and asked who wanted lemonade. They never let me forget that."

But then it happened. Their contact at Anthem Blue Cross & Blue Shield returned a phone call. And really listened. Crunched some numbers and signed on the dotted line. What a day that was.

"Patrick went out and bought cigars that probably cost more than the deal," Peter chuckles.

These days are different. As though that first sale opened the floodgates, McDonald's, Allstate, Century 21 and Verizon Wireless have signed on. HTM has an inventory of thousands of school systems in several states, and the total continues to grow.

"We will soon have given back about $2 million to high schools," says Peter. "You can't imagine how good it feels to cut a check to a school in need."

Family is still of utmost importance to everyone. "Our cousin is in charge of the Dallas office," says Jake. "And he's working with *his* cousin out there."

In addition to the hospitality of Queenie and Tim, the company's first landlords, the HTM partners have enjoyed plenty of family support. Patrick's father shared his experience as a small-business owner at the startup stage. "And the desk in my office is his," says Peter. Brother Rory, the St. Ignatius assistant athletic director, "has been our school-side adviser forever." And the eldest brother, Tim, handles the company's insurance needs and sits on its board of advisers.

While the team has scored several touchdowns, no one's getting cocky. It's still early in the game. Peter admits to the occasional sleepless night, but things are getting better all the time.

Business doesn't dominate the conversation when the guys get together socially, says Regan. "We're starting to have kids, so that's what we talk about mostly."

They all agree that the time spent in close quarters in the Fitzpatrick attic didn't have an adverse effect on their relationships. They might squabble now and then about day-to-day events, but it never lasts.

"We grew up in a family of five boys. You don't hold a grudge," says Peter.

Have Fun!

Some people take the career philosophy "do what you love" to **extremes.** Mountain climbers, lion tamers and competitive eaters come to mind — but how happy would you be to *play* with toys all day? The Goods are doing just that, by combining a child's sense of **adventure** with a very adult-size helping of business **know-how.**

Sid Good, right, and his brother, Bruce, mix kid's ingenuity with adult business sensibilities.

T he focus group loved the concept. It was a new Polaroid product, and the test audience was thoroughly taken with it. Never mind what the thing actually did; what held the group so entranced was something they had never seen before: the black-and-white prints used for convenience in the prototype. They were, after all, 21st-century kids, testing out the wares of a 21st-century kind of company.

Good Marketing Inc. is based in an overgrown former schoolhouse in Cleveland's Little Italy neighborhood that's been converted into an unlikely but hip mix of art galleries, commercial space and apartments. The Good brothers have filled their digs with well-ordered displays and overflowing stacks of sample toys, novelty candy, yummy foods and kid-friendly merchandise they conceive, test and help bring to market.

There's the wet-and-wild Water Blast Hockey, a disgusting display of Gross Outs adhesive strip bandages, a colorful lineup of Fossil Pop suckers and Candy Catcher costumes for the hands-free accumulation of Halloween booty.

No wonder the backs of the guys' business cards read, "Have Fun!" Or that the Goods call themselves, in a trademarked sense, "The Kid Experts." Or refer to their office as "the clubhouse" on phone messages.

Sid, 49, is company president. He worked in brand management at Frito-Lay Inc. and last served in new-product development and as brand manager for the toy manufacturer Hasbro Inc.

He started Good Marketing in 1989, and his wisecracking brother came on as the vice president three years later. Bruce, 42, brought years of experience from his tenure as an account executive at Young & Rubicam Inc. and DDB Needham.

The brothers began as consultants for child-friendly manufacturers such as Hasbro and The Little Tykes Co., helping them determine the viability and positioning of new products. They'd conduct focus groups, putting a bunch of kids in a room with new toys to see what happened.

"Kids tend to like anything," Sid explains. "The question is, how long do they play with it in relation to whatever else new is out there? '

Good Marketing still consults for toymakers, but the most creative aspect of the brothers' work is in product development. Pitching ideas that come from their expanding network of freelance inventors, or trying to turn their own concepts into marketable toys. They also handle packaging, product naming and logo design.

It beats selling potato chips.

Both brothers have been involved, in one way or another, with selling packaged goods for adults. But, as Sid discovered, "There's a big difference between expanding existing lines [packaged goods] and creating new brands [toys]."

Their never-ending goal is "to continually try to fill the pipeline." It doesn't leave much time for boredom.

The Royal Potty is one of the Goods' best sellers. "If you get a couple of years out of a product, you're doing well," Bruce says, "but this has been selling for four years now."

The Fisher-Price product filled a void in the marketplace. "The training potty market was boring, not fun for parents or kids," he says.

While most of us would have missed the notion that such a market could even hold entertainment value, Sid thought up a few bells and whistles for the staid product line. The Royal Potty is a training potty chair that, to put it delicately, emits an encouraging fanfare of music whenever something passes its sensor, located halfway down the detachable plastic bowl. The sensor is the electric eye you've seen open supermarket doors your whole life. The brothers just put it to new use, and they're still reaping the royalties.

The Goods know their audience.

Water Blast Hockey represents a fresh slant on an old idea. It's a summertime yard game that connects to a hose and invites kids to pump gallons of water, theoretically at a puck, but ultimately at each other, just like those super-soaking water guns that have sold for years. And yet it's different enough to get featured on "The Today Show" and enjoy a four-year lifespan.

The need for new ideas never ends. It's not the kiddos or their parents who kill most marketed toys after a couple years. The retailers get bored easily. It's a challenge and an opportunity. On one hand, they can invest time, money and energy into a product that, though successful enough to earn shelf space, gets yanked before paying much back in royalties. On the other hand, think "Royal Potty."

The major manufacturers' own R&D people concentrate on "refreshing the brand" of existing moneymakers. For instance, coming up with new clothing lines, household items — and even boyfriends — for spoiled superstars like Barbie and her friends.

"They're really dependent on their outside inventor network to continually bring in new ideas, new concepts, new inventions, new technologies," says Sid.

So how do they make inspiration strike time after time? By reading everything from general news and culture magazines such as *Time*, *Newsweek*, *People* and *US News & World Report*, to the hip business and lifestyle publications *Wired*, *Fast Company* and *Metropolis*. They scan parenting magazines and spy on their end users by poring over everything Nickelodeon. They look to Japan and elsewhere for ideas that haven't yet crossed the ocean.

Creating innovative, challenging products gets harder every year. What did you think the last time you visited a toy store to pick up a gift for a 10-year-old? Were you surprised by the selection?

"The industry calls it KGOY," says Sid. "Kids getting older younger." Children are putting away their dolls and action figures at younger and younger ages; the 4-year-old wants what her 9-year-old sister has, and the 9-year-old thinks she's a teenager.

These days, the Goods are pretty excited about an innovative plastic that turns colors and softens in warm water, then hardens under cold water. The idea is that creative users across a wide age range can mold their own action figures like clay.

GOOD MARKETING INC.
Entrepreneurs: Brothers Sid and Bruce Good
Founded: In 1989 by Sid Good, who brought his brother in four years later
Employees: 2

"You can essentially make your own toys," says Sid.

Chalk it up as one more way to fill the pipeline.

5

DOING IT

THEIR WAY

Sugar and *Spice* and Everything Nice

There's Pat Catan, and
then there's Pat Catan.
How do you *make a name*
for yourself when your
dad's already **cornered**
the **market** on it?
By following in his footsteps
and **creating** a dynasty
of your own.

Patrice Catan is what you might call a dynamo.

Since she was a young girl, she has worked side by side with her father, Pat Catan, in the family business, Pat Catan's Craft Centers. She started out creating flowers and floral arrangements. But her urge to design was irresistible; soon she was churning out headpieces, veils and jewelry. Then cake toppers. Party favors. Anything white. Her work was taking a definite turn toward the "I do" industry.

Eventually she began to kick around the idea of an entire bridal fashion world, manifested through the creativity and vision of a designer, namely, her. "I told my dad about my idea and its unique concept," she remembers, "and he said, 'Go ahead.' So that's what I did."

Did she ever.

She opened a small bridal shop in the back of one of her pop's craft stores. It grew steadily through the years, outgrowing its space and kicking the craft store down the street. "Once I had the entire space to work with," Patrice says, "I expanded this business to the vision I had always had for it, the direction I felt it needed to go."

She dreamed big; bigger than New York City's legendary Kleinfeld, bigger than Paris fashion week. She built the largest bridal salon in the nation. Period.

It's nothing short of 54,000 square feet, an emporium with 65 dressing rooms, 27 seamstresses (every one of them a patternmaker by trade), a tuxedo rental shop, a runway and seating for fashion shows, even a café to refresh weary best friends and overwhelmed spouses-to-be.

The shop has the most concise concept Patrice has ever seen in a bridal salon. "Everything done here is done for a reason," she notes. "Everything is purchased by me — the gowns, the accessories, the favors. So everything in this building coordinates. Other people have dabbled in creating something like this, but they don't have the diversity we do."

Patrice takes pride in her vision. That means more than just selling dresses; it's the concept of selling an entire package to brides-to-be. She meets her clients, then considers their body size and shape *and* their personality before recommending dress styles and accessories. More style consultant than shop clerk or buttoned-up businesswoman, she wants her brides to leave feeling that they got the complete package, not just a dress. The store is laid out in a way that invites women to browse for all their needs. It's all part of the grand vision of the grand dame herself.

"We probably have more than 1,500 wedding gown samples, 1,000 mother's dresses and special occasion pieces and 900 bridesmaid's samples," says Patrice.

CATAN BRIDAL & FASHIONS
Entrepreneur: Patrice Catan
Founded: 1987
Employees: 45-60 depending on the season

"There is nothing to compare it to. Not even Klenifeld's has this much."

It's possible that no one at Kleinfeld works as hard, either. Patrice comes to work at her salon every day of the week. When she arrives, she travels the store department by department to check in with staff and put out fires, then interacts with customers to see what's moving and what's not. "Patrice keeps a good pulse on everything that's happening in the store," says Dan Hearns, operations

Patrice Catan has been the go-to gal in the bridal industry for almost 20 years now.

manager and a faithful employee of 20 years.

She is nothing if not hands-on: She sells dresses and accessories, helps check in deliveries, waters the plants outside and has even been seen taking out the garbage. "She believes in being on the front lines," Dan says.

She also believes in letting employees (45 to 60, depending on the season) handle their own departments and responsibilities. "She's not afraid to let us run our own affairs," says Dan. That Patrice — just like her dad ...

She is the oldest of four children, and all of them work in the family business. As each sibling came into the company, they all worked in different aspects of the business. "My father was the type of person to let each of us do our own thing and grow within the company," she says. "I think it works because we have a lot of respect for our father and what he created. We felt strongly that we needed to stick together as a unit. Plus, it's a lot of fun. Most family businesses cannot say that."

In fact, one of Patrice's favorite things about being in a family business is getting to be around her family all the time. She calls it a luxury. "I've watched all my nieces and nephews grow up. They're like my own children." But there is a drawback to such an arrangement. "You have to be very careful. You have to learn to step back, and when it's not your division, keep your mouth shut."

Her father, one of seven children, grew up in McKees Rocks, Pa., a coal-mining town. "He never had anything," says Patrice. "He taught us that family is first and, no matter what, you always stick with family. Even when you're mad."

He was a wildly successful entrepreneur, and, according to Patrice, the father of the craft industry in the United States. "He was a pioneer that created the craft industry as we know it today."

Pat started his craft empire by selling wood-pulp flowers. But that was only the beginning. Next came foam rubber and tissue paper flowers, then plastic flowers and, finally, silk flowers. Today there are 29 Pat Catan's craft stores throughout Ohio and Pennsylvania.

Oh, and one humongous Catan Bridal & Fashions in Strongsville.

Long live craft, and brides, and the creativity of the Ohio Catans.

One small part of the biggest bridal salon in the nation.

A Perfect *Balance*

It's one of those timeworn
mantras the gurus of entrepreneurial
success *love to spout*:
Don't go into business with
your **best friend**!
Is there any hope for **buddies**
who have a great idea?
Just ask Barb and Margie ...

Barb Brown and Margie Flynn are all-American girls. They met on a double date with guys who eventually became their husbands. They stayed fast friends through their transition into the real world, pursuing work in the same field, getting married, having kids, doing it all together. And then, something happened. Two things, actually.

While Margie worked part time at National City Corp., Barb worked from home, "going bonkers and freelancing." Her husband came home after work one day to find Barb still in her pajamas. When she told him that "Sesame Street" had been particularly funny that day, he pulled her into the living room. "I love you, but you're losing yourself," he said. It was a wake-up call that happened at the perfect time.

Margie called Barb soon after to say she was being pushed too hard in her part-time position — could Barb come on board? It was a coincidence, it was fate, but whatever it was, it signaled the beginning of a friendship rooted in the outside world *and* the working world. They were initially skeptical about working together, afraid it might throw their friendship out of balance.

But they went for it.

They chose a job-share arrangement for its continuity; the job could be performed end-to-end — same job, different time. "We had to be in very close communication, and in those days there was no e-mail, just faxes," says Barb. "We talked probably for an hour or two every night just to transfer knowledge." The arrangement was a huge success. Margie and Barb job-shared for six years and were promoted three times as a team, ultimately to vice presidents and co-managers of corporate communications at National City.

"And at the same time, we were able to keep balance with our family lives," Margie says. "That was our original goal with working part time, and we achieved it." Another goal was to preserve their friendship, which they basically used as a tool to excel. "We knew how each other thought, knew our work ethics and pet peeves," says Barb. "We transferred all that into our job share."

Then, toward the end of 1995, National City began outsourcing. "We were getting in some good work, and some not-so-good work," says Barb. "We saw stuff that we thought we could do ourselves, and do it better." At the same time, the company was going though change, and the team began to realize they had reached their peak.

What do you do when you're at a jumping-off point? Jump.

Barb suggested that they start their own company. She had always seen herself

Margie Flynn, left, and Barb Brown mix a heartfelt approach with shrewd business sense.

running a company and was eager to go; Margie was a little more reluctant. "Barb was definitely the risk taker," Margie says. And though she was hesitant, she would be swayed. "Barb felt so strongly that we could do this that I began to see and share her vision."

Their boss was very supportive of the idea, even agreeing to hire them to do some of the same National City projects they had been handling as employees. So BrownFlynn Communications opened its doors with tons of work, doing general corporate communications and organizing an annual videoconference for National City. Essentially, National City made up its client base — and the workload was so extensive that there was little time to break away and actively grow the business. "We were happy with their revenue," says Barb, "but we had no time left over to diversify."

Then, an intervention. And a divorce.

While reading *PR Strategist*, Barb came across an ad for a consulting company called Recourses. Something about it caught her attention. She decided to call them in. "The ad asked questions directed to creative firms, and they were the same questions we had been asking ourselves," says Barb. "I got the idea that this service was just what we needed."

Hiring the consultant had a huge impact on where BrownFlynn ultimately ended up — he helped them focus on business development by suggesting they divorce each other. "From our days as job-sharers we were so used to doing the same job at the same time," says Barb. "It felt right to be operating BrownFlynn that way." But once they split up, it freed time and energy to let Margie handle the marketing and business-development side of the business so Barb could oversee client account management.

At first, Margie felt lost and adrift, away from the familiarity of the profession she knew so well. "I felt like Yukon Cornelius [from *Rudolph the Red-Nosed Reindeer*], chipping away at my iceberg to set sail into the unknown." As new accounts began to come in, she gained confidence, but still felt drawn to what Barb was doing. "It took so much discipline to not let Margie get involved in my duties," says Barb. "I knew she could be such help, but I had to turn her away. That was extremely difficult."

The consultant also urged them to specialize. Two mothers? Best friends? Women with hearts of gold? What else could they choose except community education and outreach?

Today, their work focuses on building strategic communications between for-profit and not-for-profit organizations and foundations. "We had performed so many of the components that make up this kind of work," says Barb. "We found it to be tremendously rewarding." She says they looked at other options that could have made a lot more money, but, ultimately, they wanted to make a difference.

The niche they chose has helped determine not only the nature of the work they do, but the very culture of their own company. And it's something they treasure. "BrownFlynn has a heart and soul, and we're here to nurture it," says Margie. The company culture at BrownFlynn supports team activities that strengthen friendships and allow for fun and adventure as part of the work experience. Their Fanatics program offers a monthly get-together arranged by employees — a *during-business-hours* get-together. Fanatics activities have included Elvis birthday parties, jewelry-making parties and group nursing-home visits at the holidays. One very special company outing sponsored by Barb and Margie was a flight to Chicago for a day of shopping. "The Fanatics sessions are so rewarding for all of us," says Margie. The duo sees them as an opportunity to foster team building and friendship within the company.

Together, they've arrived.

"We wouldn't be where we are without each other," says Margie. They turn to each other when they reach a block, let each other know when to move on, inspire each other. "If somebody told me they were going to go into business with their best friend, I'd tell them they were out of their mind," says Barb. That said, Margie and Barb acknowledge that they have a unique circumstance. One guided by fate and faith. And certainly friendship. "We're blessed to

BROWNFLYNN
COMMUNICATIONS
Entrepreneurs: Barb Brown and Margie Flynn
Founded: 1996
Employees: 6 employees, 2 principals and a team of associate consultants

have each other," Margie says. They call it a codependency, but a balanced, healthy one.

All-American girls: At home, they're the mommies, the tidy-uppers, the fixers, the everything and anything their family needs them to be. At work, they're doing it all in smart suits. And loving every minute of it. Together.

A *Change* Will Do You Good

Imagine **seeing** a business
and deciding on the spot that
it's too good to pass up.
Nevermind that it's a business
you *know nothing* about, or that
it's something completely **different**
from the career track you're on.
Scary? Maybe.
Exciting? Definitely.

John Baraona made the seamless switch from realtor to dry-cleaning whiz.

John Baraona was 32 years old when he found his calling. Better late than never, eh?

"It just happened," he says nonchalantly. "I was a real estate broker looking for a business to buy." He discovered a laundromat in Fairlawn, bought it along with a couple of Don Mor Cleaners stores, and before you can say "six starched shirts," he became the unofficial dry-cleaning king.

For John, changing careers from real estate to dry-cleaning was really no fuss at all. The only fuss about making the change was the business name he chose, and how he decided to treat his customers. Other than that, he just had to learn everything from scratch.

No problem.

Today, John has built Fussy Cleaners into a 17-unit chain servicing 40 communities throughout Northeast Ohio. Fussy Cleaners charges a little more for its services, but despite that, the company has made a name for itself by going the extra mile; it offers, for free, lots of extras that the other guys don't do at all. Same-day service? No problem. Repair hems and sew on loose buttons? No problem. Pick-up and delivery service at home or office? No problem. The business even has personalized bags for regular customers who don't want to

The Fussy Cleaners

wait in line for drop-offs.

If they sound like innovative services conceived by someone with a taste for the business, someone who grew up in the industry and had a vision for what a dry cleaner should be like, think again. Much of John's insider knowledge came from the front-line employees who were already running the business. People who met John and took an instant liking to him.

"I felt comfortable in dealing with people and the employees who were running the business, so I was never nervous or worried about making the change," says John. "As we grew, I was also able to use some of the relationships that I had developed in the real estate industry in terms of finding the right locations for new stores."

John's interaction with the existing employees, allowing them to contribute and take responsibility for their ideas, helped forge fiercely loyal employees. He also borrowed some basics from other retail industries, "things like the aesthetics of the stores, the cleanliness of our operations and making sure that the equipment we were using was the most up to date," he says.

Like the computer system that keeps track of individual orders for more than three months after a pickup — it can tell John who waited on the customer when the order was picked up and even the worker who pressed the item.

As his business grew, John learned to watch shifting consumer trends. While you might think that would mean keeping up with fashion, or at least the fabrics used in those fashions, it actually came down to his customers.

"It really has more to do with the daily habits of the consumer," John explains, "and how often they visit the dry cleaner versus not going. It used to be that people got dressed up to go to the church or synagogue. Today they don't. It used to be that office casual day was once a week, now it's every day. Responding to those changes and having to adapt has been our biggest challenge over the last five to six years."

Adapting to change means keeping a finger on the pulse of day-to-day operations, which John is able to do through his front-line associates. By offering extensive training, flex time and above-industry-average benefits, John has been able to maintain a loyal work force, which these days exceeds 130 people. Some people in his organization have worked at Fussy Cleaners for more than 20 years, and more than 100 have been with him for five years or longer. Nearly all of his managers have advanced from a counter or presser position.

"I think my biggest accomplishment is being able to grow the company with the associates who work here," says John. "To continue to give them challenges so they can move up through the organization, and to provide opportunities for them."

And his employees have reciprocated.

"Our people here have given me the opportunity to get involved in the community by affording me the time to participate in various philanthropic activities," John says.

Fussy Cleaners is particular about the communities it serves. The headquarters is lined with various testimonials and awards from various local philanthropic organizations. The community efforts show a creativity to match the company's services. It has made contributions to area Metro Parks and provided free dry cleaning for unemployed people going on job interviews. The company has been recognized as a Pacesetter (a designation awarded by the United Way to companies that raise money to "improve the quality of life for all Greater Clevelanders") and was a sponsor of the Akron Zoo's Holiday Lights exhibit — not to mention the company's regular support of public radio and television, among many other charitable endeavors. All of which, for John, just seem natural.

"It's not all about business," says the real estate guru turned dry-cleaning kingpin. "Whether they're your customers or your associates, business is really all about people."

An *Awakening*

Van Roy Coffee was a happy
company, perhaps a tad on the
complacent side, used to doing
things the way they'd always been
done. Then one day the new kid
showed up, bearing an odd resume
and a tiny coffin. The company
would *never* be the same.

Jeff Miller knows beans.

Jeff Miller was a primo ad exec back in the 1990s. He sold air space for Cleveland FM radio staples including WNCX, WQAL and WGAR, moving up the ladder until he was soon in position to become the next national sales rep for WGAR, a station on the top of the charts at the time. Poised for large-scale success, married to a woman with California dreams, Jeff saw only sales and San Diego in his future. But fate intervened in a most unexpected way.

Jeff hadn't married just anyone; he chose the girl with coffee in her blood: Susan Schanz, heir to The Van Roy Coffee Co.

OK, so "heir" might be a little extreme. Susan's brother, John Schanz Jr., had been a staple at the company for most of his life, while Susan fled the Midwest to work in an art gallery on the West Coast. Coffee was the last thing on her mind, and her marriage to Jeff only secured the belief that she wouldn't return to the family business.

John Sr. had other plans for his daughter and son-in-law. Susan and Jeff thought they were making an innocent visit when they flew to see Susan's parents in Florida in the winter of 1995. But their world turned upside down almost immediately.

"I wasn't in their apartment for more than five minutes when Mr. Schanz popped a question," says Jeff. John Jr. had a lifetime of experience on the operations side of the business, and with John Sr. making the move to retirement, he needed someone to take over the marketing side.

"He was looking for someone with fresh blood, someone with a sales mentality," Jeff explains. "The company had always made money, but sales were slumping."

After an afternoon of introspection on the beach in Florida, Jeff accepted the challenge, and left his career in radio to step in as president and CEO of Van Roy Coffee.

His first move was to clean house, eliminating positions that were redundant or overstaffed. It wasn't the most inviting path.

"I'm not going to say it was easy, because it wasn't," he says. "I was an outsider coming into a closely knit family business. My first job was to make [John] feel as comfortable as possible."

Jeff realized that John's skills in manufacturing and operations could help grow the business if there was an equally strong person on the marketing side.

"John's strength has always been in manufacturing, keeping the plant running, because that's where he was brought up," says Jeff. "I just told him, 'You run the back of the house, and I'll run the front.' And that seemed to work."

For everyone else, Jeff brought out his coffin-shaped idea box. When his employees told him, "That's how we've always done it," or, "That's who we always use," Jeff would resolutely point to his box and tell them, "You know where that goes: Right in the coffin."

Jeff continued to plow through the ritualized processes in the company, attempting to eliminate the 1950s and '60s mind-set that had kept the company from realizing its full potential.

"I told the people here that we weren't going to change the fundamental products we offered — great, fresh coffee and good service — but we were going to change our systems, like the way we stored inventory," he says. "When I came here, they were still doing things in paper bags. It worked well for years, but in order to make it grow, we had to move forward."

THE VAN ROY COFFEE CO.
Entrepreneurs: Jeff Miller and John Schanz Jr.
Founded: In 1930 by John Schanz. His son-in-law Jeffrey Miller stepped into the presidency in 1996, teaming with John's son John Schanz Jr. to run the company.
Employees: 9

The savvy former ad exec also refocused the company's selling strategies.

"The business was approximately 90 percent focused on restaurants," he says. "They had gotten away from the businesses that had made them strong, the institutional and office coffee services. So we decided to go after those elements of the business." That meant new equipment, something Van Roy couldn't afford.

No capital for new machines? No problem.

"We went to our equipment suppliers and asked for extended terms, whatever it took so we could open these new accounts," Jeff says. "You just don't know what you will get until you ask, and our suppliers were very eager to work with us."

Then he went after existing accounts. He saw the risk involved in signing deals with new restaurants that might not last, so he changed the way Van Roy dealt with clients.

"We didn't want to offend existing restaurant customers, but we did need to better protect our receivables," says Jeff. "So I proposed that all new restaurant accounts, of establishments that had been in business less than 10 years, would come in on a COD basis. We didn't offend existing customers, and as we built the business our receivables were protected."

He also eliminated overhead, moving the business out of its historic headquarters in Ohio City and into a new facility on Spring Road in Brooklyn Heights, a move that no doubt saddened many in Ohio City who were used to the scent of freshly roasted coffee wafting through the neighborhood. As a part of the move he also cut back on the company's consumer store operations.

Talk about stepping on a few toes.

Ten years into his leadership role at Van Roy, Jeff is finally feeling good about the future of the company. While he handles the advertising and marketing ends, John Schanz is the operational manager of the business, and they've created a solid partnership focused on constantly improving the company's competitive position.

They're exploiting two lucrative niches in the coffee market, industrial and office sales, while maintaining the restaurant business. The company is leaner in its operations, and more profitable.

"I like where we are at right now," Jeff says. "We're in a position to grow."

And those California dreams he and Susan once shared? For now, they're memories.

"I caught the coffee fever, and I haven't looked back since," he says.

Like Father, *Like* Son

The name Mort Tucker has, for more than *50 years*, meant breathtaking **aerial** photography of the changing Cleveland **landscape**. Mort got his photography business off the ground, and his son Howard took it to new heights.

Howard Tucker has spent a lifetime documenting the faces and places of Cleveland.

Mort Tucker was a photography hobbyist in the 1950s when he met and married the daughter of local photographer Herb Rebman. Coincidence? Perhaps. Mort didn't appear to have any ulterior motives — he had recently completed an accounting degree at Ohio State University and acquired a job in downtown Cleveland at Cole National.

There was just one problem: He hated it.

So after six months of corporate Cleveland, he came to work for Herb as business manager of his photography studio. That's right: business manager. He still didn't plan on getting involved in the shooting side of the biz.

But his hobby inevitably came in handy for his father-in-law, and eventually Mort started going on photo assignments.

By 1962, Mort was immersed in the industry. Herb died that year and Mort found himself pseudo-owner, along with Herb's son, daughter and wife, of Rebman Studios. For almost a decade Mort struggled with the "too many cooks in the kitchen" syndrome, and finally struck out on his own with Mort Tucker Photography, a studio space of 3,000 square feet at 16th Street and St. Clair Avenue.

By this time, Mort's talent was well known and well respected in Cleveland, and the demand for corporate and advertising photography was growing. He was soon able to expand to 10,000 square feet. Work began coming in from department stores including Halle's and May Company, which were locally owned and producing their own ads. Mort set up on-site studios at the department stores to shoot merchandise for brochures and newspapers.

Life was good.

Mort's son Howard was a teenager by the time Mort Tucker Photography really came into its own. He grew up on the periphery of the business, making photography a hobby just like his old man had. He still owns the first camera he ever used, a 35 mm Nikormat that his dad gave him as a bar mitzvah present. He used that little camera just for fun. "I didn't shoot anything too great," he remembers modestly, "but there were a few things I shot as a kid that probably had a little artistic value."

He had enough talent and know-how to assist on shoots as a teenager, and had young legs perfect for helping with deliveries. "I was 14 years old, wandering downtown by myself," Howard says. He got an insider's view of the growing city. "I began to know all the buildings, stopped and read plaques, took my time. It was fun, something none of my friends were doing."

When Howard turned 15, Mort gave him a nicer camera and license to shoot some buildings downtown. At 17, he got his first professional job, a business portrait for a local company. Then came the '80s, and an explosion of interest in stock photography. Cleveland was experiencing a rebirth, and everyone wanted local photos for brochures, books, newspapers and magazines, even for personal art. The Tucker studio was well established, and the bulk of the work came there. And some of the photos they were scooping up were young Howard's.

Business was booming, but like his father Howard wasn't that interested. He followed in Mort's footsteps and headed to OSU for a business degree.

He hated it.

Two years later, he was following his father's footsteps right back home, to the family business.

MORT TUCKER PHOTOGRAPHY
Entrepreneur: Howard Tucker
Founded: In 1971, by Mort Tucker. His son Howard took over in 2003.
Employees: 5

He started back at the shop as a jack-of-all-trades, shooting everything from catalog shots to interiors and exteriors, but his old interest in the city never went away. He continued to be fascinated with the city's architectural transformation.

As each new building in Cleveland went up, Howard was there, making a photographic record of the construction process. "One of the first buildings I shot was BP Tower," he remembers. "We were hired to go in every three weeks and take four shots on every floor. That's 50 stories." He also saw, and shot, the construction of skyline favorites such as Key Tower and One Cleveland Center.

To get the best shots, Mort and Howard had to scout locations from helicopters, airplanes and lofty rooftops. For self-described acrophobics, it was a stomach-turning prospect.

"Believe it or not, my father has always been afraid of heights," says Howard. "But the act of holding a camera somehow chased that fear away every time." They scouted locations together with Howard perched at the edge of skyscraper rooftops trying to find the best angle while Mort stood 30 feet behind him and warned him not to fall. "Maybe he thought a magical gust of wind on a clear blue day would sweep me from the roof," Howard says.

But Howard has his own peculiar phobia: Cessna airplanes. "I hate them," he admits. "They bounce you around like a roller coaster. I get nauseous every time I go up in one." But, just like his dad, when he put a camera in his hand the sickness would go away. "Go figure," he says. "My dad and I really get caught up in what we do."

These days, Mort's caught up in retirement, leaving Howard to run the family business. Just like his dad, he's doing things his own way. But where 50 years ago Mort was on the cusp of corporate and advertising photography, today Howard is reaping the benefits of tapping technology early.

"Back in the '90s, when digital equipment started coming in, there was a huge learning curve," Howard says. "Since I was the young guy just coming in, I was involved with keeping up with technology."

The studio started computerizing everything from book work to imaging to retouching. Because he was in a family business with his father running things at the time, Howard was afforded a lot of time to learn the technology. He spent hours, entire days, just playing around with it and learning it inside and out. By the time other studios caught up, Howard had 15 years of experience and knowledge under his belt. When it came to digital technology, Mort Tucker Photography was decidedly ahead of the game.

The technical revolution changed the studio. Though photographers still go out on shoots, the time it takes for follow-up work — running prints, getting work to the client — has been reduced from days to minutes. The studio now requires less space and fewer employees to do the same amount of work. It uses computers for everything.

Howard says that, ultimately, this is a great business. "Every day is different. We thrive on crazy, last-minute rush jobs." Maybe the business hasn't changed for Howard that much over time after all. Once rushing around downtown making daily deliveries for his father, now he rushes around downtown getting last-minute jobs to grateful clients. "I get huge satisfaction from people saying, 'Thank you, you saved me,' " he says. "And I love to see my clients smile at the work we do." Not bad for a couple of businessmen-turned-artists.

Outwork, Outdo, Outlast

There are the so-called "book smarts" and then there are "*street smarts.*" Growing up in urban Cleveland is a good way to learn the latter. As a kid on the East side, Ben H. Williams Sr. learned the first of many lessons that didn't come from any book, and they made him what he is today: a survivor.

It was a Thanksgiving weekend that few Clevelanders would ever forget. It started out like any other Thanksgiving, except that it was unseasonably warm. In what had become a tradition on Cleveland's East side, Case played Western Reserve at Shaw Field. Turkeys and hams were roasted. Families sat down to dinner. And that evening, a gentle snow began to fall.

What few Clevelanders realized that Thanksgiving night in 1950 was that a tightly wound low-pressure system was working its way up through Appalachia. It was a vicious snowstorm that would drop more than 17 inches of snow in 24 hours, drifting in places to more than 3 feet. The next day, the streetcars were unable to move because of the drifting snow. Tanks from the Ohio National Guard worked their way through the streets of Cleveland, delivering milk, food and relief to thousands. And on Frank Avenue on the near East side, a father and son dug their small Jeep CJ Tow Truck out of the driveway to help motorists stranded in the snow.

"It was one of those Jeeps they actually used during World War II," says Ben H. Williams Sr., owner of Ben's Auto Body Specialists on Carnegie Avenue on Cleveland's East side. "My dad had put a boom on it and we went all over to tow cars."

That morning, with nothing moving, Ben Williams watched as his dad broke the small tow truck free from their driveway.

"I don't know how many cars we towed that day, I just remember watching my dad work," says Williams. "But I can remember that I was so small that when I stood in the snow it was up to my chest."

Ben's father, Ben F. Williams, was always prepared to do for himself and help those around him. And his spirit was infectious. In 1943, when Ben F.'s town was dying along with the coal industry and steel was up and coming, he moved his family from Kentucky to Cleveland and bought not one, but three houses. They were for his brothers.

"Each of them ended up owning their own businesses," says Ben. "Each of them became an entrepreneur." Including, of course, Ben's dad. The original Ben opened a service station on East 55th Street and Short Scovil Avenue, followed in 1949 by an auto body shop near Euclid Avenue and East 40th Street.

That shop would eventually become Ben's Auto Body Specialists once Ben H. came on board, although that wasn't in his father's plans. He wanted more for his son: a college education, the key to success and upward mobility.

Ben H. Williams Sr. is constantly on the lookout for ways to improve his business.

"Instead of going to … East Tech for vocational training, I went to John Adams for college preparatory," says Ben H. "I worked in the auto body shop during high school, but I was going to college when I graduated. It was my father's dream."

But love and life intervened. "I got married and started a family right out of high school," Ben says, "so I adapted." He came back to the family shop and turned his energy toward learning everything he could about the auto body business. He learned the industry from the ground up, starting as a technician repairing accident-damaged cars.

The little shop cruised along for years until the elder Ben started experiencing heart problems in the early '80s. He survived quadruple-bypass surgery, but after more surgery and a stroke, Ben's dad died in 1983. Ben found himself with a successful business that could sustain his family and a few employees but had little chance for growth.

Cupid had nothing to say about it this time: Ben went back to school, enrolling in a management course on the advice of a friend. The classes gave him the edge he needed to complement a skill he already had: Working with cars damaged in accidents.

He learned that networking was crucial. He started getting involved with organizations and associations affiliated with the auto body business, such as the

American Service Association and I-Car, and began to realize that the auto body business was actually several different businesses, each with its specific profile, each filling a niche.

"I tried to match my talents with one of those specific market niches," says Ben. He began working with insurance companies and found there *was* opportunity for growth in his field.

But to stand out, it took the old Williams work ethic. Ben and his staff just outworked the competition. They took their business and services to places that repair shops had barely considered.

For instance, the shop itself is kept clean inside and out, and each vehicle that comes into the dealership is detailed before it's picked up by the customer.

"A lot of people have the image that an auto body shop is dirty and dingy," says Ben. "We work hard to dispel that image."

Ben's shop is also one of just a handful in Ohio that provides its customers, via the Internet, with real-time shots of the work being performed on their vehicles.

"And that was something I got from a 20-member industry focus group that I was involved with," says Ben. "It gives our customers a real-time look at the work being performed on their vehicles. But it's also cut down on the number of calls we have to answer from people asking questions about their vehicles.

"And it's also helped to market our business as well. A lot of these people are checking up on their vehicles while they are at work, and a lot of their co-workers are watching what we do. So when they get into an accident, we get a lot of business from them as well."

Sales figures increased fivefold between 1997 and 2001, "And we haven't even scratched the surface of where we can be," says Ben.

These days, Ben is looking forward to his own retirement, when he'll hand the company over to his son, Ben Jr., who is president of the company.

Ben Jr. also came back to work for his dad at the auto body shop. But first, he fulfilled a Williams-family dream: He graduated from college, with a degree in business and marketing from the University of Boston.

> BEN'S AUTO BODY SPECIALISTS
> **Entrepreneur:** Ben H. Williams Sr.
> **Founded:** In 1949, by Ben H. Williams Sr.'s father, Ben F. Williams. Ben H. Williams Sr. took over in 1983.
> **Employees:** 9

"I'm sure he will take the business further than I ever could," says Ben H. Williams Sr. "After all, this is what he was trained for."

The *Nineteenth* Hole

Don't we all want to work hard,
get rich and **retire** young?
Apparently, spending time at a **vacation**
home in Tahiti isn't up everyone's
alley; there are some entrepreneurs
out there who just *can't quit.*
Take Jim Skoch: As his retirement
present, he **bought** himself a golf course.
This is a working retirement if
there ever was one.

It's the story of a guy who was on the back nine of his career — a long, lucrative and satisfying career calling his own shots as the owner of an aluminum company. He decided to get out of the game, but wanted to stay active and occupied somehow, continue to use his business smarts. Then he discovered a way to have it all. He bought a brand-new golf course — StoneWater Golf Club. What better way to ease through the dessert days of a career, taking it easy on the links and hobnobbing with the country-club set. Right?

Not exactly.

It was a move Jim Skoch took very seriously, and it was way more work than you'd think. Sure, days spent at the golf course have their advantages over those spent toiling in an aluminum factory. But business is business, and whether it's the recreation industry or the manufacturing industry, there is hard work to be done, as well as challenges to face, people to manage and problems to solve. Some leisurely retirement. But the truth is, Jim wouldn't have it any other way.

Jim is a career entrepreneur. He caught the bug while caddying as a young man at Westwood Country Club in Rocky River. "I was always thrilled to listen to stories of small business owners," he says. "And I wanted to be one myself."

Just out of school with a degree in business and finance from Baldwin-Wallace College, Jim took a job as manager in the aluminum business at Cuyahoga Smelting. That gig was a bit like running his own company: He managed the aluminum division for its parent company, Rossboro Manufacturing. "I had completely green roots at that time," he says. But he learned the operation, learned the importance of listening to people and learned a lot about leadership.

At age 29, after working at Rossboro Manufacturing for seven years, he left to acquire a company called Rock Creek Aluminum. He understood and knew the aluminum business well, and if he was ever going to take a risk, this was the time to do it. "When you do something like that, you never really think of failure," he says. "You think, 'What do I have to do to make it work?' "

Jim owned, ran and grew Rock Creek Aluminum for close to 20 years, then in 1995 decided to sell it and move on. Time to retire? Not yet.

The man who made a career out of running corporations went back to the place where he first realized he could run corporations: the golf course. A good friend, Gregg Foster, knew that Jim was looking for another business that was totally unrelated to aluminum. Gregg had started StoneWater Golf Club, an 18-hole course in Highland Heights. It was like a light bulb went on over their heads. Just after opening in 1998, Gregg sold the course to Jim.

"When I took it over there were definitely some hurdles," Jim says. The course had garnered plenty of accolades and recognition, locally and nationally, and had earned the critics' praises, but it needed a clubhouse to really take off. It was completed in 2002, creating an atmosphere that lets StoneWater continue to grow its business and membership and contributing to a significant increase in revenue.

The personal transition for Jim, from running an aluminum company to heading a golf course, was actually one of the smoothest parts of the move. "I play golf and have always enjoyed it," he says, "so I had knowledge of golf." Plus, in any business, entrepreneurs encounter the same basic problems and challenges, 95 percent of which are people problems.

A little bit of work, a little bit of play is the Jim Skoch method of retirement.

Jim says it's how he deals with employee issues and how well he listens to customers that were the big issues at both his former job and his current one. "In that respect, running StoneWater is no different than what I was doing before.

"If you listen to the people you work with and you listen to your customers, I guarantee you'll be successful," he says. And that correlates with his ideas about leadership. "Leadership is nothing but listening to the people that are giving you information, the people you work with," Jim says, adding that nobody really works for him at StoneWater — he and the staff work together. "My job is to give them the tools to do their jobs," he says. "All a good leader does is provide the ability for employees to be successful. They take care of the rest."

StoneWater Golf Club

The state of the course at StoneWater these days is a testament to the hard work and dedication of Jim and his staff. "It's really something to start a golf course — and we're basically in our infancy here — that gets ranked 28th in the nation [by *Golf Digest*] and that has an opportunity to host

STONEWATER GOLF CLUB
Entrepreneur: Jim Skoch
Founded: By Gregg Foster in 1996; Jim took it over in 1998.
Employees: 50-100 depending on the season.

a nationwide tour event [the Cleveland Open]," Jim says. "That's very satisfying for all of us. We're proud of what we have here."

And for Jim, success is a direct result of a positive attitude. "I believe that there's nothing I can't do," he says. "And that today is the best day of my life." In dealing with the good and bad aspects of owning a business, it's attitude that will make the difference.

So Jim has created a new way of retiring to the golf course. This version comes with more hours, headaches, stress and hard work than just hitting the links with your buddies. But it also has its share of fulfillment, success, achievement and pride. That beats a birdie any day.

6

WITHOUT
A NET

The Art of *Business*

Ah, the **romance** of the artist's
life. Parisian art colonies, summers
painting by the seaside, glitzy
openings filled with rich patrons. ...
It's a **pretty** picture, all right,
but far from reality in Cleveland's
art scene. To make it here, you've
got to be **tough**, have a plan
and wear a strong pair of pants:
You're going to be flying by
the seat of them quite a bit.

Vincent van Gogh lived off his merchant brother. Mark Twain never met a bad investment he didn't like. And there's hardly a famous rock band in history that hasn't been ripped off by its management and left to face "Behind the Music."

Put simply, the artsy crowd is rarely confused with the entrepreneurial class. Creativity and commerce aren't supposed to meet or even take the same train to work. Heck, it's practically undignified for a right-brainer to know how to balance a checkbook, much less analyze a profit-loss statement.

"To be quite candid, I've seen six galleries close in the last year. They aren't the most stable businesses," says Roger McAndrews, a pottery exhibitor and one-time gallery owner himself.

So what's an artistic entrepreneur supposed to do?

How about hold down three jobs and work a blue streak while endlessly networking and contributing to the advancement of several local nonprofits?

It's working out for Hector Vega.

Vega, 42, and his wife, Monica, own a café that sells art. Or an art gallery with Pablo Picasso (turkey, ham, roast beef) and Georgia O'Keefe (hummus, roasted red peppers, artichokes) on the menu.

Like most challenging art, their business defies the norms of categorization.

"It's designed to survive," he says of Artefino Art Gallery Café. "When we have a slow day in the café, maybe I'll sell a work of art. It balances out."

Vega's space has anchored the first floor of the Tower Press Building since the summer of 2004. The looming twin towers and castle-like visage of the red-brick structure are cool and edgy, a natural draw to area artists. Inside, the café is high ceilinged, light and airy, an inviting slice of menu and culture. White-washed walls offset colorful acrylics, jewelry pieces and pottery that come and (Vega hopes) go. Local artist Todd Volkmer's pop-art portraits of Hector and his wife draw the eye upward, where the black ceiling and track lighting further jack up the hip quotient. The sleek, white tables — a dozen or so — seat hungry guests and starving artists alike.

It's an ingenious concept, says Volkmer, known simply as Todd V. "If [customers are] just going into a café for a sandwich, there's less price intimidation."

For a man who loves to network, Vega's approach is decidedly low key. During a lunchtime interview, his dark eyes can't help roaming the small room. He politely excuses himself to greet the regulars, then returns with a smile and an apology.

He recites phone numbers from memory, and his cell phone rings repeatedly.

Hector Vega rarely has time to take a breather at his own cafe. "I always have a lunch meeting," he says.

During one call, Vega listens intently, then says, "Yes, I might be very interested, but I'm meeting with someone right now. Can I get your name and number and call you back?"

It's called deal-making, an art form in itself. Vega connects with clients, with artists who ask him to sell their work on consignment and with civic activists and do-gooders who want him to run their benefits. The Vegas host several of these events at their café and cater on-site to others. He sits on local arts boards and organizes his own festivals and fund-raisers.

"My edge in business," he says, "is by being very resourceful and not afraid of hard work."

And, true to artistic form, he goes his own way. It was the starving artist inside him that opened Artefino, after he "got tired of paying 50 percent commissions to gallery owners," he says. He designed the place himself and traded art for architectural services.

In addition to being co-proprietor of the café, Vega has a full-time job as construction manager for the Cleveland Metropolitan Housing Authority. And at nights and in the wee hours of the morning, he completes his own predominately large-scale corporate- and privately commissioned paintings.

"It's nonstop energy," says Volkmer of his friend. "I can't believe how hard he's pushing. That's really where his success comes from."

There's another source, as Vega is quick to point out. "My biggest failure in life is not meeting my wife sooner," he says of Monica, who he's been married to since 2004.

Vega met the former Monica Lukez at — this should come as no surprise — the Tremont ArtFest. "She blindsided me," he says with a slight smile.

The two have much in common. Hector came from Puerto Rico with his mother and three siblings when he was 8. Monica emigrated from Italy at the age of 2. Both settled in Cleveland.

Monica also shares her husband's work ethic. She earned bachelor's degrees in psychology *and* sociology and has a full-time job as a guidance counselor and admissions consultant for the Cleveland Institute of Electronics. Her art is culinary: She designed Artefino's menu.

Monica shrugs off the fact that her workday can begin as early as 6 or 7 a.m. to set things up at the café. "And then I come back here after work to close up and bake."

Altogether, that's five jobs for the Vegas.

"It's a sacrifice," she admits. "But it *will* work."

You can hear the struggle in her voice and see the tenacity in the couple's approach to life. Just how long can you hold down as many jobs as there are days in the workweek for the sake of self-expression and entrepreneurial freedom?

"I love the business of art as much as the art itself," Hector says. Despite the hours and the odds, he wouldn't change a thing.

And in the end, he always has his first love.

Chances are, you've seen his work. There's a geometric vibrancy to his signature pieces, the colorful neighborhood cityscapes teeming with urban life. "He's very people-friendly," says Monica. "He likes to be around people, and they gravitate toward him."

> ARTEFINO ART
> GALLERY CAFÉ
> **Entrepreneurs:**
> Hector and Monica Vega
> **Founded:** 2004
> **Employees:** 5

Running a restaurant is often identified as one of the riskiest business ventures one can undertake. It's about as sensible as trying to make a living as an artist.

"It's scary. It's always scary," Hector admits in a reflective moment. "But if I lose it all, they can't take my creative mind away."

Catch a *Wave*

Young entrepreneurs, gather 'round. We're going to tell you a **true** story about the business world. You won't see **Bill Gates** starting in the garage and winding up a multigazillionaire; you won't hear about **Oprah** and her decades-long bosom-buddy relationship with millions of viewers. This is the real deal: A career of **ups** and *(gasp!)* **downs**.

We know the celebrated rags-to-riches format. You're supposed to struggle, but only in the early days, before forward momentum launches you to stratospheric heights and you buy yourself a Hummer, put your wife in a Ferrari and use "summer" as a verb, as in your family's penchant for "summering" on the Riviera.

What's not supposed to happen are sleepless nights *after* making *Inc. Magazine*'s list of fastest-growing privately held companies in America. You're not supposed to so radically reconfigure a successful company that most of your old employees quit because they no longer understand it. And it's unheard of that after a decade in business you go from 189 employees one year to 65 or so the next.

"Jokingly I say that over the last 16 years I've done a startup, two transformations and a turnaround. It just all happened to be with the same company," says Len Pagon in an attempt to describe the rocket-ship-ride/crash-and-nearly-burn experience of running a technology company over the last couple decades.

It's been a madcap existence for the 40-year-old founder, president and CEO of Brulant Inc., the IT consulting and business-management firm he started in his 20s. He's spent the bulk of his career leasing new offices and picking up awards for fast-track growth, but has also spent significant time closing offices and struggling to meet payroll.

"It was just uncertain times," says Alistair Bailey, a senior consultant and seven-year Brulant employee, of the most memorable down times. "But we weathered the storm when a lot of competitors were going under."

Here's a test: If your palms sweat while reading the following employment numbers, you should not give up your day job.

1989: One employee

1992: 20-25 employees

1998: About 180 employees in four offices

1999: About 65 employees

2002: "Low 30s" employment

2005: 125 employees, with another 30 needed immediately

Does it make sense? Not really. Individuals who don't have the self-confidence and steely composure to ride out the bad times, knowing that the wave that just crashed overhead will inevitably recede — eventually — should pay attention to the Len Pagon story. If it scares you, so be it.

These days, Brulant (the word is Scottish and means "brilliant, scorching,

Len Pagon is known around the office for keeping his cool and playing a mean game of paintball.

sizzling, hot") is once again on fire. It's in what Len refers to as "hypergrowth mode," desperate to recruit new talent. Desperate to the point of offering hiring bonuses and a referral cash-bonus program with the grand prize of a 42-inch plasma-screen TV for the employee who can deliver the most hirable bodies. You'd think it were 1999 all over again, and no one had ever heard the term "dot-com bust."

Len comes across as earnest and unflappable. No more likely to gloat over the current situation than he was to fly off the handle in response to past crises. He uses the expression "catch a wave" a lot, referring to the importance of seeing the next tech trend before it crashes over you. He happens to be on top of one this time, which is certainly better than sucking for air and choking on water. The best strategy for survival, he's learned after nearly two decades in business for himself, is to see that wave coming before it hits you.

Easier said than done, folks.

How many of us had heard of the Internet before the late '90s? Trying to keep up with the hurricane speed of technology is hard enough as a consumer. But what if your business existence depended on being able to not only keep up with but also stay a step or two ahead of the digital curve?

Len Pagon got involved in technology as a teenager. He attended Case Western Reserve University but while his schoolmates were enjoying beer, cold pizza and sleeping in late, Len was working a full-time job.

His tech know-how got him hired at 18 as a technician for American Endoscopy, a medical-imaging company.

"Within a month," he says, "they saw that I could do a lot more than that. By the end of the summer I was a kind of pseudo-engineer."

Len redesigned a disinfecting machine and, by the time he was 19, had traveled to 40 states on business while simultaneously pursuing a degree in electrical engineering.

He never did get a job like other grads. Len worked as a consultant for American Endoscopy and for his own biomedical clients. When he was asked to troubleshoot a clunky user interface for an imaging-management system being introduced with little acceptance to hospital ERs, Len came up with a friendlier Windows-based and Mac-based interface and a mouse-driven graphical operating system.

"That's how the company, which I called NewMedia, started," says Len. "For the first couple years we didn't even know what business we were in."

He accepted whatever tech challenges came his way and realized that Macintosh was the hot platform of the moment. He formed a relationship with Apple that got him tons of business from the computer maker's clients who needed custom business software. Suddenly he was working for the likes of TRW, British Petroleum, Lubrizol, Nationwide Insurance and GE Turbo Engine Division.

But by 1992, it became obvious to Pagon that Windows was going to be the dominant platform.

"We had 20 or 25 employees by then, mostly Macintosh-zealot software engineers, very creative but not very presentable in corporate America."

Moot point, because the hardcore Mac loyalists had no intention of sticking around when the switch of platforms was made.

From 1992 to mid-'93, he remembers, "80 percent of the staff turned over."

The mass exodus didn't change the company's growth patterns.

"From '89 to '98, we grew at a compounded growth rate of about 80 percent a year," says Pagon. "We were on the 'Inc. 500' [list of fastest-growing companies] for three consecutive years, and were the fourth-fastest growing in Ohio in '96."

By 1998, there were four Midwestern branch

BRULANT INC.
Entrepreneur: Len Pagon
Founded: 1989
Employees: About 150

offices. A board of advisers and a new executive team were in place by the late '90s.

Pagon says, "I knew the Internet was going to be a big deal in '95 and started talking about it at staff meetings by '96." By this point the company was a regional programming-development house, writing custom client server systems for Fortune 1,000 companies.

Len had started to hire a management staff, but there wasn't much depth.

"I had IT people running branches rather than businesspeople. The biggest thing I had missing was management talent." It would turn out to be a costly problem.

"The first year we couldn't get traction" was 1998, he says. "We weren't making enough progress on this Internet opportunity."

Len sold off all the branch offices, in most cases letting his former people go with the purchasers.

The problem, says Len, was that the company had gotten too big to turn on a dime, like it had years earlier when switching platforms. The tidal wave known as the Internet had risen unexpectedly and almost swamped the whole company.

But spirits stayed as high as could realistically be expected during that time, says Judy Borlin, the client-relationship manager and another longtime employee, thanks in part to the boss' candor.

"[Len is] very down to earth, and very honest with everyone," she says. "We trust him. There was never a time when he was like, 'Everything's going fine.' "

Today, everything really is going fine. Pagon found a new focus and now works with corporations in financial services, health care, life sciences, and consumer goods and retail. The company recently gained 8,000 square feet by moving from Garfield Heights to new headquarters in Beachwood. And one lucky employee is going to reap the benefits of Brulant's latest upswing in the form of a plasma TV.

Keep on Truckin'

Throughout the 1970s and '80s, William Hall was one of the many minority entrepreneurs struggling to overcome **racism** in the business world. Today his son, Brian, presides over a family company that owes its success to the **efforts** and **tenacity** of the previous generation and the vision of the current one.

When William Hall started out in the mid-1970s, it was just him, his brother Horace and a truck. Industrial Transport Inc. has grown from one truck to more than 100. William and Horace handed the presidency over to William's son, Brian, in the mid-'80s. But they almost didn't have a company to hand over.

"I watched my father get involved in a number of industry issues," says Brian. Mainly, William and Horace grappled with deregulation of the trucking industry. The industry was heavily regulated in the '70s — small trucking companies couldn't get licenses and couldn't compete with the big businesses. Minority companies were even further behind.

"There were no minority trucking companies who could get licenses in the late '70s," Brian remembers. It was a case of industrial racism. And with the regulations in the trucking industry, if you weren't licensed, you couldn't get work. Because of personal connections, Brian's dad was able to beat the system and get a few jobs. From there, satisfied customers and word of mouth kept his business going.

But William didn't stay quiet about the state of the industry. Instead, he became part of a national consortium of trucking companies who, with Ohio Sen. John Glenn and Rep. Parren Mitchell of Maryland, fought in Washington, D.C., to deregulate the industry. Brian went to some of their conventions. "I remember in college giving a business communication speech after having just been to a conference," Brian says. "I spoke about deregulation and the fact that only one-quarter of 1 percent of all the dollars our government spent on transportation was spent with minority trucking companies. That was institutional discrimination."

The group was eventually successful, and in the '80s the industry was deregulated. The value of a license disappeared, and the playing field leveled … a little.

Industrial Transport was still a small company trying to leverage itself for jobs against the big guns of the trucking industry. That was when Brian entered the picture.

INDUSTRIAL TRANSPORT INC.
Entrepreneur: Brian Hall
Founded: In 1977 by brothers William and Horace Hall. They made William's son Brian president in 1984; he officially purchased the company in 2000.
Employees: About 250

Brian Hall was immersed in his courses at the University of Cincinnati, working toward a degree in architecture and helping the family business during school breaks. His father never pushed him to join the company, and Brian had never given it much thought, until he started looking a little closer at the documents he was working on. "I realized, based on the invoices I was seeing, how large the business was and that there was actually an opportunity for me here," he says.

Brian asked his father for a job, and even offered to change his degree to be a better fit. He had to

Brian Hall followed in his father's and uncle's footsteps by caring about his community along with his industry.

make up for lost time, but by attending school over summer break he was able to graduate only one quarter behind his class — with a business degree.

Brian graduated on a Friday in August, loaded, drove and unloaded his U-Haul over the weekend and started work first thing Monday morning. "It was a great opportunity for me and I was excited about it," he recalls. "I was looking for a place [where] I could someday be my own boss."

Just four years later, William and Horace handed Brian the presidency of Industrial Transport. Over the next decade, the men would grow the company to 27 locations nationwide.

It was tough. Even after the trucking industry was deregulated, Brian recalls encountering an inherent belief that they couldn't do it, because their clients hadn't seen other African-Americans doing it. "You look at things that are publicized," he says, and the only African-Americans he saw in the spotlight of success were either entertainers or athletes. Plus, he explains, "We didn't have the capital that some of our large competitors who had a 100-year start on us had. There was great difficulty in that."

But Brian, William and Horace worked hard and focused on the service side of their business, so people were saying good things about them. They got a lot of business through word of mouth and excellent references. "That helped us overcome," Brian says. Today, Industrial Transport boasts such big-name clients as Apple, Ford and General Electric. In 2000, Brian officially purchased the company from his father and uncle.

President Hall hasn't forgotten the past. In 1996, he founded the Presidents Council, a group of some of the largest African-American-owned companies in town. The group has several missions, one being to develop a business relationship with the entire business community to be a part of the region's economic development. "We want to see the region grow like everyone else, and we're a part of that growth. So we need to be a part of the discussion," Brian points out. The council is a way for them to get to know the CEOs of the major companies.

Is it working? "I would say over the last 10 years since we've been formed, we've been involved in the leadership of almost every economic development organization or movement around town," he says.

The President's Council also collaborates with Baldwin-Wallace College to create an emerging-entrepreneur program for African-American business owners. Brian compares it to a mini-MBA program that helps business owners learn how to be successful.

All of Brian's initiatives are focused on instilling a sense of togetherness in Cleveland's African-American community. After all, he says, minority entrepreneurs may not think they need any help, but "they need to realize that someone thought to open the door they might be going through. We have to be at least a little politically active. We have to keep fighting."

'Are You In or Out?'

What would you do if someone asked you that question, and he wasn't just making dinner plans? Would you **commit** yourself to a town you left behind and a company you knew was in trouble? In business, there is no *crystal ball* — and sometimes all you've got is your instinct.

Michael Summers is proud of the range of products his company started producing when things got tough.

"**A**re you in or out?" the voice on the phone asked. "I have to make some plans. What are you thinking about?"

It was a call Michael Summers had been expecting.

"My dad was 60 years old then," Mike recalls. Retirement age. "I asked for a day to reflect. But that call set in motion a series of decisions which would change my life forever."

William Summers, Mike's dad, wanted him for the presidency of the family business, Summers Rubber Co. It was a potentially lucrative offer to lead a major company. On the other hand ...

Mike had just graduated from Northwestern University with his MBA. He was living a big-city life in Chicago, enjoying the hustle and bustle of working right in the middle of everything, experiencing the challenges of a job in the fledgling computer-software industry.

He'd found a girlfriend at Northwestern, Wendy, and proposed. She accepted, but, looking to jump-start her own career, Wendy jetted to New York City and got a job as a consumer marketer for Planter's Peanuts. "We did our share of flights back and forth to see each other," Mike remembers. They had both chosen their paths in life — and they didn't involve Cleveland.

Meanwhile, Summers Rubber Co. had just 13 employees, and its outlook could only be described as troubled. All of North America, not just Northeast Ohio, was in the midst of a dramatic industrial downturn. Steel was still the focus of Summers Rubber's customer base, and steel was not prospering in Northeast Ohio.

Besides, there were few consumer marketing positions in Cleveland for Wendy if the couple did attempt the move home. And why move back to a city that was the butt of national jokes when they were living in two of the greatest cities in the U.S.?

So, of course, they did it.

"I decided I would make a serious mistake if I didn't at least try," Mike says. "This was a business leadership opportunity. It was what I was trained for. I enjoyed business and this was a marketing-oriented company. That is something that particularly interested me as opposed to finance or engineering."

Mike joined his father's company in 1980 and married Wendy soon after.

"Our family joke is that we met halfway in Cleveland," he says.

Professionally, the couple was taking a big risk, but before she returned to town, Wendy got a position with The Sherwin-Williams Co. as a product manager in Cleveland.

"And as it turns out, the group I was with [in Chicago] were wiped out by the coming of the PC," says Mike. "I probably would have been nimble enough to make the shift over to the PC side, but, nonetheless, the computer industry was blindsided by its own future."

Summers Rubber was getting a little blindsided itself, and for the fresh-faced businessman in Mike, that presented a unique opportunity to prove what he was capable of.

"Immediately upon my arrival, the company started heading south in terms of both sales and performance," says Mike. "I had to explain to everyone that it wasn't my fault — but I don't think they believed me."

> SUMMERS RUBBER CO.
> **Entrepreneur:** Michael Summers
> **Founded:** By Michael's grandfather William H. Summers in 1949. Mike took over from his father, William M. Summers, in 1984.
> **Employees:** 57

Summers Rubber didn't sell to the automotive industry directly, but a lot of the companies it worked with did. When the American automakers lost some ground to the Japanese auto industry in the 1980s, Summers Rubber found itself indirectly affected in a big way.

"When they caught a cold, we caught the flu," Mike says of the auto industry problems.

Realizing its customer base was under serious pressure, father and son knew the company needed to diversify.

"At that point my dad was very anxious to leave the company," says Michael. "He had been in the business for 40 years and was a little tired of it. But he was supportive of taking a risk, and understood the dire straights of doing nothing — that it didn't make sense."

"If we're going down, we're going down swinging," the elder Summers says. "I'd rather be shot as a wolf than shorn like sheep."

William Summers' statement ushered in an exciting time in the company: An entrepreneurial experience that was more robust adventure than board meeting boring. Mike's first year with the company included plenty of risk, speculative investment and necessary expansion. All of that, plus no pay.

That's right: In 1981, when Mike first started and the company was in trouble, father and son gave up their salaries.

Summers Rubber expanded its customer base, "everything from liquid, gas or solid to acids and ice cream," says Mike. "Wherever there was a need to process material, whether it was jam or oleum, we would fabricate the flexible portion of their operations using our hose, hose fittings, expansion joints or other products."

The company struggled through 1981, but saw a light at the end of the tunnel.

"That first year scared the heck out of me," says Mike. "But 1982 was a little better. We had reduced our costs to meet market conditions, and we got the sense that we were going to survive. In 1983, things actually got better."

Mike officially took over the reins at Summers Rubber in 1984, becoming the third generation of Summers to run the business. Under his leadership, the company embarked on an aggressive expansion, buying facilities in Mansfield, Findlay, Dover, Marietta, Eastlake, Akron and Newcastle, Pa.

"But I don't really consider myself an entrepreneur," he says. "I am, after all, the third generation of ownership of this company, so I had a running start — which was a definite advantage.

"What I was given was the opportunity to take a solid foundation, work it hard, and then take it further than it has ever gone. And that we have been able to do."

Ice Cream Wars

In a **nation** of conglomerates and
multibillion-dollar megacompanies,
a successful **regional** chain that's
not on the verge of selling out
can be hard to find.
Meet Pierre's.
The Cleveland-based company is
staying true to its **hometown**
and its rich history, and it's
finding success. Plus, a little
decadent custard never hurt sales …

Ohio born and bred — Pierre's has been churning out ice cream from its Cleveland-based plant for more than 50 years. Today, the founder's daughter, Shelley Roth is at the helm.

W hen you think of Pierre's French Ice Cream Co., words like "new" and "regional" hardly come to mind. Pierre's is everywhere and it's been around forever — hasn't it?

That would seem to be the case to lifelong Northeast Ohioans. But the fact is, the co-founder of the company we know today, Sol Roth, is still alive, though retired. His daughter, Rochelle (Shelley) Roth, runs the 140-employee company from the sleek distribution center and corporate offices the company carved out of a rundown section of Euclid Avenue in 1995.

After serving in World War II, Sol Roth took a peacetime job driving a dairy truck. Royal Ice Cream, a modest frozen-treat shop, was on his route.

"There were hundreds of little ice cream shops like that, where they actually made it in the back and sold it out front," says Shelley.

Sol discovered one day that the joint was for sale. "He was able to grab a few dollars, and the guy who owned it let him pay for it in installments," says Shelley.

He continued to sell most Royal Ice Cream for on-site consumption, but also

Pierre's French Ice Cream Co.

started to test the waters with sales to area restaurants and a handful of retailers.

The ice cream business grew in America like a lot of industries — through the determination of enterprising young folks who sunk their teeth into a trend or new technology and hung a sign in a window.

Many of these small ice cream shop owners began thinking like Sol and focusing on distribution. None strayed too far from home since refrigerated transportation was in its infancy.

"There were literally scores of these producers," Shelley recalls. "All of the big dairies would make their own ice cream."

But that was back in the day. How many mom-and-pop carmakers, bike plants or textile producers did you recall seeing on your drive to work this morning? Royal Ice Cream faced tough competition. Lots of it.

To enhance efficiency, the company shared a new production facility with Pierre's French Ice Cream starting in 1950. Pierre's had sprung to life just like Sol's. Pierre's Ice Cream Shop opened on East 82nd Street and Euclid Avenue in 1932 and had similarly expanded into wholesale distribution.

The two companies merged in 1960, when Sol acquired Pierre's and took its brand name. He gradually expanded the product line into sherbets, sorbet and other frozen goodies. The company took over the Harwill Ice Cream Co., another major rival, in 1967.

It now "owned" Northeast Ohio.

Shelley got involved in the family business at an early age. She traveled around with her father, delivering ice cream samples in the mid-'60s. She was his "little buddy," she says.

But it wasn't for her. She earned her business degree at the University of Michigan and started at the marketing department of Atlantic Records in New York City in 1978. A year later, her brother opted for medical school rather than the family business and Sol was about to lose a senior member of his management team. It was time for "little buddy" to return home, and what she found was a rapidly changing market. Pierre's was the last ice cream company left in Cleveland, and around 10 to 15 frozen-treat makers were competing for nationwide sales. By the early '80s, even those holdouts were being eaten up.

"There is so much consolidation going on," says Shelley. "Nationally, there are probably about 15 brands that have been bought by Dean Foods," an industry giant.

The result is a war that's taking place daily in the freezer cases of supermarkets and big-box retailers across America. It's even a challenge on the home turf. While

Pierre's suffers no lack of name recognition locally, "it's an ongoing challenge to get the full array of products into a retailer," Shelley admits.

Outside the company's prime marketing area, the company's brand recognition shrinks. It does all right in Columbus and areas adjoining Northeast Ohio, and has some customers in surrounding states. But while it's known and respected as a regional brand to industry insiders, Pierre's is a stranger in a strange land to outside shoppers. That's a problem.

"If you're not the No. 1 or 2 brand, you're at risk of being dropped," says Shawn Sullivan, the company's vice president of sales.

That's after paying the upfront slotting fee to claim a spot on the shelf. In many cases, Pierre's will sell well, but a new buyer will take over and find they can get a higher slotting fee from a newcomer.

Shelley and her company face the challenges by constantly updating flavors, product lines and technology.

"Everything but the quality has changed over the last 10 or 15 years," she says. "If my father came in today and said, 'Shelley, fill me in,' he wouldn't believe the changes."

Today, Pierre's French Ice Cream offers more than 200 products and flavors. The company has responded to changing tastes with low-fat and sugar-free lines.

"You always have to reinvent yourself because retailers get bored," says Shelley. "They'd rather replace a moderate success with something brand new."

Pierre's also produces private-label brands for smaller companies on the East Coast ("I'm hoping that working for their brand will broaden the opportunities for ours," she explains), and distributes national brands.

The company's efforts haven't gone unnoticed. Among its many awards is an accolade from 2001: The Authentic Frozen Custard was named Best New Ice Cream by *Esquire* magazine.

And while all around them ice cream producers are being gobbled up by the big guys, Shelley is sitting comfortably in her headquarters, a Cleveland operation that's just one mile from the company's original storefront. She's not going anywhere, unless it's to the freezer for her favorite Pierre's flavor, "chocolate, chocolate, chocolate!"

PIERRE'S FRENCH ICE CREAM CO.

Entrepreneur: Shelley Roth
Founded: Sol Roth bought Royal Ice Cream in 1932, and merged with Pierre's in 1960. His daughter Rochelle (Shelley) Roth gradually began assuming leadership starting in 1980.
Employees: 140

A LITTLE
ADVICE

"There is no luck. You make your own luck. It's the result of what you do and the hard work you put into it seven days a week, 24 hours a day. I believe there's nothing I can't do, and that today is the best day of my life."

—*Jim Skoch (StoneWater Golf Club)*

"You don't want to boil the ocean. Pick your niche and stick to it. Then you can decide to go sideways once you have built the business into something you can rely on."

—*A.J. Hyland (Hyland Software Inc.)*

"You can't do it all yourself. That's why you have to treat associates, employees and customers with respect."

—*John Baraona (The Fussy Cleaners)*

"You have to be willing to make a mistake, learn from it, and move on to the next risk. Once you stop taking risks, you stop growing."

—*Barb Brown (BrownFlynn Communications)*

"Don't tamper with a business that's successful by getting upset about the little things. It's not worth it."

—*Patrice Catan (Catan Bridal & Fashions)*

"If you find the right kind of people doing the job, you'll find the results are quite stunning. You also want people who share your values. You need a like-minded staff. Ultimately, they are the ones who will help your business grow."

—*Pat Conway (Great Lakes Brewing Co.)*

"We designed this business to be successful under the worst-case scenario."

—*Alan Glazen (Glazen Creative Studios)*

"Always be preparing, and don't ever give up. Then when opportunity finds you, be ready to move."

—*Brian Hall (Industrial Transport Inc.)*

"As an entrepreneur, you can't go wrong by tapping into more senior, experienced people."

—*Mark Kuperman (Johnny Applestix)*

A Little Advice

"Being an entrepreneur means more than wanting to be successful. You have to love what you do — that starts it. But then you have to use your head."

—*Adele Malley (Malley's Chocolates)*

"I think it's always a good idea to run your company as though you were positioning it for sale."

—*Jeff Miller (The Van Roy Coffee Co.)*

"It's a tricky matter of selling yourself, getting someone to believe in what you can do, and then delivering it."

—*Clinton Morgan (Morgan Packaging)*

"If you bring on good people and always deliver, and you're focused on the right target market — a market that's growing — you're going to outperform the market."

—*Len Pagon (Brulant)*

"There is always an opportunity for innovation and something new as existing retail organizations get bigger and more homogenous. The consumer is always looking for something exciting and new."

—*Alan Rosskamm (Jo-Ann Stores Inc.)*

"To me, an entrepreneur has some basic qualities. For one, there is a reasonable amount of risk tolerance, perhaps even a high risk tolerance. So if the worst happens, they can deal with it and move forward. Then anything above failure is a victory."

—*Michael Summers (Summers Rubber Co.)*

"Networking is, for me, the key to any small business, to any business, period. If you can't network, if you can't get out there and receive thoughts and ideas about how to run your business, you're just not going to make it."

—*Ben H. Williams Sr. (Ben's Auto Body Specialists)*

The Quotable

Entrepreneur

"We don't hold hands."

—Phil Alexander (BrandMuscle Inc.) on his confidence in
his employees and the freedom he grants them

"When we first got into this business, a lot of people thought my brother and I had the IQs of artichokes because it was a bit unrealistic."

—Patrick Conway (Great Lakes Brewing Co.)

"There are the brotherly fights."

—Peter Fitzpatrick (Home Team Marketing) on the reality
of going into business with siblings and a close friend

"Cleveland gave us a chance to go from nothing to high up on the ladder in half a lifetime. I don't know if we could do that in a community that wasn't friendly to entrepreneurs."

—Alan Glazen (Glazen Creative Studios)

"As kids get older, it doesn't matter so much what parents think."

—Sid Good (Good Marketing), on making toy and
personal product buying decisions

"The only way it will fail is if you give up."

—MaryAnn Hanson (Hanson Services)

"I have a pretty broad taste range. Like my grandfather used to say, 'I'll eat anything that doesn't eat me first.' "

—Tom Heinen (Heinen's)

"In the old days, people would call a week ahead. Now they call 10 minutes ahead."

—Norm Heinle (The Sausage Shoppe) on increased customer demands

"It's sort of like being married. We had to — and still have to — work at it and be sure to keep communication channels open."

—Mark Kuperman (Johnny Applestix)

"I'm a techno geek. I'm interested in how technology can solve the world's problems. And now I know a thing or two about getting it to market."

—Carol Latham (Thermagon Inc.)